RALPH THE BAKER

⚜ NEW ORLEANS RECIPES ⚜

RALPH WILLIAMS

83 press®

83 press®

83 Press
2323 2nd Avenue North
Birmingham, AL 35203
83press.com

ISBN: 979-8-9899185-1-5
Printed in China

RALPH THE BAKER

⚜ NEW ORLEANS RECIPES ⚜

RALPH WILLIAMS

DEDICATION

To my amazing wife, Sarah,

This cookbook is a tribute to you and your unwavering support. Behind every recipe and video shared lies your dedication and creativity. From the early mornings of recipe-testing to the late nights of video-editing, you have made this culinary journey possible.

Beyond the camera, you're my partner and my rock. You've always seen the good in me and cheered me along in any crazy idea I had. Your encouragement and support have fueled my passion and helped me overcome any challenges along the way. I'm truly grateful for everything you do.

Sarah, this cookbook is more than just a collection of recipes; it's a testament to our shared passion, dedication, and love. Thank you for being my guiding light. Here's to many more delicious adventures together.

With all my love,
Ralph

To my RTB family,

None of this would be possible without you. Your support and enthusiasm have been the driving force behind every success I've achieved. From the first video to the never-ending "butter slams," you've been with me every step of the way.

Your belief in me and your willingness to join me on this cooking adventure mean more than words can express. Each view, each like, and each share is not just a number but a reflection of the bond we share as a community.

You are more than just followers; you are family. Your support fuels me to continue creating and sharing my love for food with the world.

From the bottom of my heart, thank you. Thank you for being part of this journey, for your support, and for being the heartbeat of our RTB family. Together, we've created something truly special, and I am forever grateful for each one of you.

With one stick of butter, y'all,
Ralph the Baker

CONTENTS

8
Foreword

10
Introduction

12
Chapter 1: Big Easy Breakfast

30
Chapter 2: Party Time

46
Chapter 3: Soups, Stews & a Little Lagniappe

70
Chapter 4: New Orleans Classics

94
Chapter 5: Carnival Time

116
Chapter 6: Backyard Cookout

140
Chapter 7: Seafood Favorites

162
Chapter 8: Easy Family Dinners

186
Chapter 9: Savory Pastas

210
Chapter 10: Holidays in New Orleans

226
Chapter 11: Crescent City Sweets

252
Recipe Index

254
Acknowledgments

FOREWORD

I remember the day I met Ralph like it was yesterday. On just a random afternoon 20 years ago, our paths crossed in a way that felt like fate. He was working on his car at my neighbor's house while I was driving down the street, and our eyes locked as I passed him. That evening, Ralph came over to introduce himself. From that moment on, we were inseparable. I knew by Ralph's vibrant personality and kind heart that our lives would be full of adventure.

Ralph is not just a husband and father; he's the heartbeat of our family. His kindness, dedication, and unwavering love light up our world every day. Whether he's cooking breakfast, sharing stories, or pranking the kids, his love knows no bounds.

In the spring of 2020, Ralph took a leap of faith and began sharing his baking and cooking skills online. Little did we know that it would lead to such incredible success. From his first hesitant upload to the thriving community he's built, I've watched with admiration through it all. I've always known Ralph was destined for greatness, and I'm so happy the world can experience it as well.

While Louisiana culture is just his average way of life, Ralph learned from his audience how unique it is to the rest of the world. Our food is deeply rooted in traditions, family bonding, and celebrations; it's basically in everything we do. The memories that are created with loved ones are all tied into the dish of the day. When Ralph realized this isn't a universal experience, he was shocked. He began dedicating his platform to showing that Louisiana, Cajun, and Creole dishes could be simple and fun. He included our children and grandchild in his videos in hopes of encouraging families of all kinds that food can bring family and friends together in a memorable way.

Ralph is more than just a social media sensation; he's also a man of integrity and compassion. He uses his platform to make a positive impact, raising awareness for communities in crisis, whether it's a hurricane, a snowstorm, or just one person in need.

One of my proudest memories is when Ralph went to Texas to help feed hot meals to families affected by the 2021 snowstorm. During that trip, he met a man who volunteered to pass out food. Ralph later learned that the man was homeless. It touched Ralph's heart that a man with his own struggles would be so eager to help others. When Ralph got home, he began sharing this man's story with his YouTube community. Ralph and his subscribers raised enough money to buy the man a car and clothes, pay his expenses, and connect him with resources to find a job and housing. It was the most beautiful experience to witness. Ralph's heart for others is my biggest inspiration.

As I look back on our journey together, I'm filled with pride and gratitude. Ralph's spirit and passion for cooking shine through in each recipe he creates. I hope this cookbook brings as much joy to you as Ralph has brought to our lives.

Here's to Ralph—the man behind the butter, the master of the kitchen, and the love of my life.

With love,
Sarah Williams

INTRODUCTION

Before I was Ralph the Baker on social media, I was working as a tree climber. It was dangerous work. Every day, you didn't know if you were going to live or die just to bring money home to keep food on the table. I'd work long hours and come home wanting to unwind, so I'd sit and watch Food Network. At the time, *Cake Boss* was popular, and it usually played when I was getting off work. I loved that show. I saw a lot of myself in Buddy Valastro. I mean, if this guy from Hoboken, New Jersey, could make these beautiful cakes, why couldn't I?

I started small, making simple layer cakes in the kitchen. I taught myself all the techniques, from piping to fondant. I remember I was learning how to airbrush for more-realistic cakes, and I didn't realize that while I was spraying the cake, the spray was getting all over the kitchen, too. Sarah, my wife, got home, and the whole kitchen was blue. I was in so much trouble! I kept learning, though. By the end, I was making these beautiful, elaborate cakes. I made a giant moving army tank with sparklers that spun. I even made a life-size poker table that was fully edible!

Cooking and baking became my favorite hobby. I know that in a lot of places, it's unusual for men to be cooking so much, but down here in Louisiana, a lot of men cook. It's not abnormal in the South to see men in the kitchen. I started at 10 years old, watching Mom and Maw Maw in the kitchen. They taught me everything I know. I wouldn't trade those days spent in the kitchen with them for anything. It gave me an appreciation for how good food can bring people together.

During COVID-19 lockdown, I decided to post a recipe video to TikTok. I closed out the app and didn't open it for three months. When I came back, the video had hundreds of thousands of views. Seeing such a positive response made me want to post more. Millions of views later, here we are, officially publishing my own cookbook.

If you've been with me for a while, thank you for the continued support. Nothing I do would be possible without you. If you're new here, I'm excited you're going to start cooking with me. In this cookbook, I gathered my favorite recipes from over the years. From social media sensations (like my Boudin King Cake Burgers on page 100) to family classics like Maw Maw's New Orleans Praline Candy (see page 240), there's something for everyone in this book. I hope you enjoy it as much as I do.

Here's to a little bit of Cajun seasoning and a whole lot of butter!

—Ralph

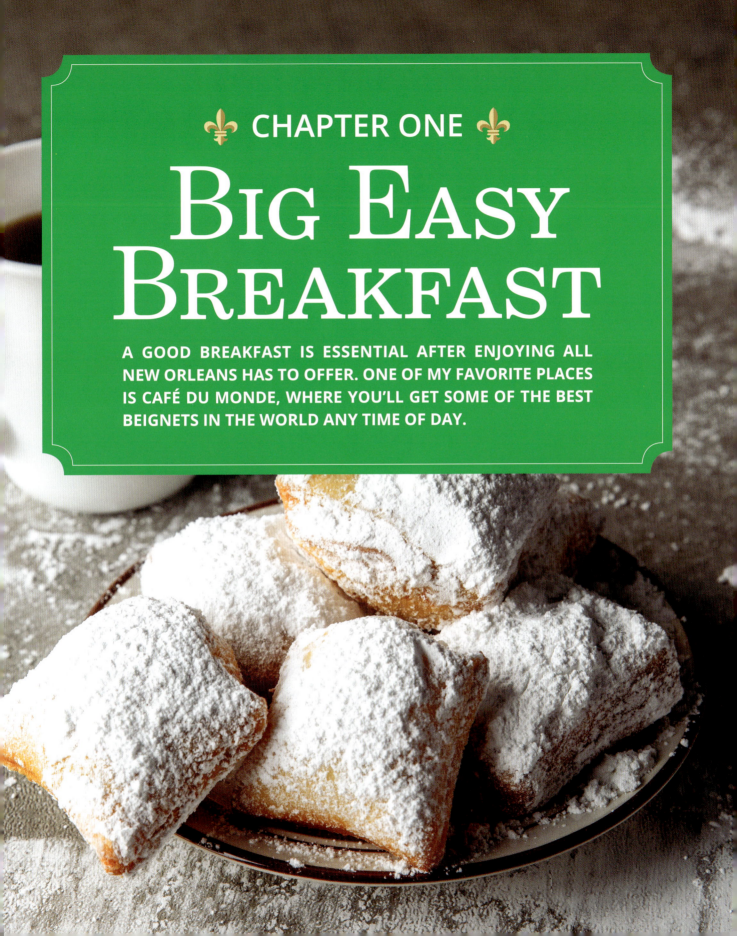

CHAPTER ONE

BIG EASY BREAKFAST

A GOOD BREAKFAST IS ESSENTIAL AFTER ENJOYING ALL NEW ORLEANS HAS TO OFFER. ONE OF MY FAVORITE PLACES IS CAFÉ DU MONDE, WHERE YOU'LL GET SOME OF THE BEST BEIGNETS IN THE WORLD ANY TIME OF DAY.

ALL FOR THE FAMILY

My life changed for the better at the age of 16 when I found out I had a kid on the way. I might have been young, but I knew I was going to do everything I could to take care of my daughter. I missed out on being a kid myself, but I wouldn't change it. Life has its way, and everything that's meant to be, will be. I'm proud that my daughter can say I was in her life and that I did everything I could for her. She might not understand all the sacrifices I made, but that's OK. I'd make them again.

Everything I do is for my family. I have a wonderful wife, five great kids, and a grandchild. I'm blessed beyond measure to get to do what I do and support them. I'm close with all my kids, and food has only brought us closer. There's nothing like sitting outside cooking with your kids, talking while you're waiting on food, to build that relationship. ⚜

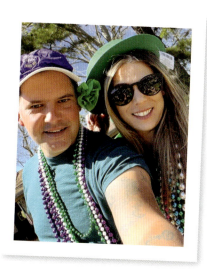

PRALINE SAUCE

MAKES ABOUT 2½ CUPS

**Whether it's with pancakes or ice cream, this sauce can't be beat.
You'll want to make extra to can and keep on hand.**

**1 cup firmly packed light
brown sugar**

1 stick (½ cup) salted butter

½ cup water

1 cup chopped pecans

1 teaspoon vanilla extract

Pinch kosher salt

1 In a medium saucepan, combine brown sugar, butter, and ½ cup water; cook over medium heat until sugar completely dissolves and butter is melted, stirring constantly. Once mixture comes to a gentle boil, reduce heat to low, and let simmer for about 5 minutes, stirring occasionally. Stir in pecans, and simmer until syrup has thickened slightly, 3 to 5 minutes.

2 Remove saucepan from heat, and stir in vanilla and salt. Let cool for a few minutes. Carefully pour syrup into a clean, sterilized jar. Seal jar tightly, and let cool to room temperature. Once cooled, store it in the refrigerator.

NOTE: *This praline syrup can be used as a topping for pancakes, waffles, ice cream, or any dessert of your choice!*

Brioche French Toast with Praline Cream Cheese Filling

MAKES 4 SERVINGS

**My oldest son, RJ, and I like to make this for the family on the outdoor griddle.
Less mess in the kitchen is a great way to start everyone's day!**

4 ounces cream cheese, softened

½ cup Praline Sauce (see recipe on page 17), plus more to serve

¼ cup chopped pecans

2 tablespoons powdered sugar, plus more for dusting

4 large eggs

1 cup whole milk

1 teaspoon vanilla extract

½ teaspoon ground cinnamon

8 slices brioche bread (preferably a day old)

½ stick (¼ cup) unsalted butter, divided

Fresh berries, to serve

1 In a large bowl, stir together cream cheese, ½ cup Praline Sauce, pecans, and powdered sugar until well combined and smooth. Set aside.

2 In a shallow dish, whisk together eggs, milk, vanilla, and cinnamon.

3 Spread cream cheese filling on 4 slices of bread and then top each with another slice to create sandwiches. Dip each sandwich into egg mixture, ensuring both sides are well-coated.

4 In a large skillet or griddle, melt 2 tablespoons butter over medium heat. Cook 2 sandwiches until golden brown and filling is warm and slightly gooey, 3 to 4 minutes per side. Wipe skillet clean; repeat with remaining butter and remaining sandwiches. Let stand for 1 minute. Drizzle with remaining Praline Sauce, dust with powdered sugar, and serve with berries.

RALPH'S TIP

Stuffed French toast can feel like a lot of work first thing in the morning. Do some things the night before to make it easier. Put together your stuffing (step 1) and egg mixture (step 2). Keep them covered and in the fridge overnight. Then, you just have to wake up and start dipping your bread.

LOUISIANA CAJUN
BREAKFAST SKILLET

MAKES 6 SERVINGS

Coated in my Cajun seasoning, potatoes are covered in cheese, sausage, and vegetables and topped with eggs. This is a great one for the family on the weekends.

1 stick (½ cup) salted butter

1 large yellow onion, sliced

1 large green bell pepper, cut into ½-inch strips

2 teaspoons kosher salt, divided

1 teaspoon ground black pepper, divided

2 teaspoons RTB Dubba-U Sauce

1 (16-ounce) package hot smoked sausage, sliced

2 tablespoons vegetable oil

1 pound small red potatoes, quartered and cooked

2 teaspoons RTB Cajun Seasoning

2 cups shredded Cheddar cheese

6 large eggs

1 Preheat an outdoor flattop griddle over medium heat. Add butter to one side of griddle. When butter melts, add onion and bell pepper. Sprinkle with 1 teaspoon salt and ½ teaspoon pepper. Cook until tender, about 6 minutes, turning frequently with a metal spatula. Stir in RTB Dubba-U Sauce. (Continue to stir onion mixture occasionally.)

2 While onion mixture cooks, add sausage to middle of griddle. Cook until lightly browned, about 5 minutes, stirring occasionally.

3 While onion mixture and sausage cook, place a 12-inch cast-iron skillet on other side of griddle. Add oil. When oil is hot, add potatoes. Season with RTB Cajun Seasoning, remaining 1 teaspoon salt, and remaining ½ teaspoon pepper. Sprinkle with cheese. Spoon sausage on top. Spread onion mixture over sausage. Crack eggs onto onion mixture. Cover and cook until egg whites are set and yolks are how you like them. Serve hot.

NEW ORLEANS BEIGNETS

MAKES 24

If you've been a fan for a while, you've probably seen me on live going to the world-famous Café Du Monde for beignets. I couldn't get enough of them, so I learned to make them at home! These are a taste of the French Quarter right in your kitchen.

1½ cups warm water (110°)

1 (0.25-ounce) package active dry yeast

1 cup warm whole milk

½ cup white sugar

2 large eggs

½ teaspoon kosher salt

7 cups all-purpose flour, divided, plus more for dusting

½ stick (¼ cup) unsalted butter, melted

Vegetable oil, for frying

Garnish: powdered sugar

1 In a large bowl, stir together 1½ cups warm water and yeast; let sit until foamy, 5 to 10 minutes. Add milk, sugar, eggs, and salt, and stir until well combined. Add 4 cups flour, and whisk until smooth. Stir in butter and remaining 3 cups flour. Cover and refrigerate for up to 24 hours.

2 In a large Dutch oven, pour oil to fill halfway, and heat over medium-high heat until a deep-fry thermometer registers 350°.

3 On a lightly floured surface, roll out dough to ⅛-inch thickness. Cut into 2½-inch squares.

4 Fry in batches until beignets pop up and are golden brown, 2 to 3 minutes, turning dough frequently during frying. (If beignets do not pop up, the oil is not hot enough.) Let drain on paper towels. Sprinkle powdered sugar over hot beignets.

Cajun Sausage Gravy

MAKES 10 SERVINGS

Talk about delicious! Pour this over my Southern Buttermilk Biscuits for the perfect start to the day.

½ pound ground breakfast sausage

¼ cup all-purpose flour

3 cups whole milk

1½ teaspoons RTB Cajun Seasoning

1 teaspoon dried sage

¼ teaspoon ground white pepper

Kosher salt and ground black pepper,
  to taste

RTB Cajun Hot Sauce (optional)

Southern Buttermilk Biscuits
  (recipe on page 26), to serve

1 In a large skillet, cook and crumble sausage over medium heat until browned and cooked through. Sprinkle flour over cooked sausage, stirring well to combine. Cook for 1 to 2 minutes to remove the raw taste of flour. Gradually pour in milk, stirring constantly to avoid lumps. Continue to cook and stir until mixture thickens to your desired consistency, 5 to 6 minutes.

2 Season with RTB Cajun Seasoning, sage, white pepper, and salt and black pepper to taste. Add a few dashes of RTB Cajun Hot Sauce (if using). Reduce heat to low, and let simmer for a few more minutes to allow the flavors to blend. Taste and adjust seasonings if needed. Serve warm over Southern Buttermilk Biscuits.

I started my RTB Seasoning line in 2020. At the time, I was selling hot cocoa bombs, king cakes, pralines, and anything else my followers were interested in. We started by mixing the seasoning blend up in our kitchen and putting it in store-bought jars with flip-top lids. The labels were simple, just "Ralph's Spicy Cajun Seasoning" on a white sticker that we had to hand-wrap around each jar. We've upgraded a bit since then with dozens of products sold worldwide.

SOUTHERN BUTTERMILK BISCUITS

MAKES 12

Cooked in a cast-iron skillet, these biscuits get a beautiful brown color on the bottom. Hit them with some extra butter to get that nice golden color.

1½ sticks (¾ cup) unsalted butter, cold and divided

2 cups all-purpose flour, plus more for dusting

1 tablespoon baking powder

½ teaspoon baking soda

½ teaspoon kosher salt

1 cup whole buttermilk

Cajun Sausage Gravy (recipe on page 25), jam, or honey, to serve

1 Preheat your oven to 450°.

2 Cut 1 stick (½ cup) cold butter into small cubes. (Or grate butter, if desired.)

3 In a large bowl, whisk together flour, baking powder, baking soda, and salt. Add cubed butter (or grated). Using a pastry blender (or fingers), work butter into flour mixture until mixture looks crumbly. Make a well in center of mixture, and pour in buttermilk, stirring until just combined. (The dough will be sticky.)

4 Turn dough out onto a floured surface, and gently knead a few times until it comes together. Pat dough until about ½ inch thick. Using a 2½-inch round biscuit cutter dipped in flour, cut dough. Gently re-form the dough scraps, and continue cutting until all dough is used. Set aside.

5 In a 10- or 12-inch cast-iron skillet, add remaining ½ stick (¼ cup) butter, and place skillet in oven until butter is melted and hot, about 5 minutes. Carefully take skillet out of oven, and place cut dough in skillet, letting biscuits touch without smashing them.

6 Bake until biscuits are golden brown, 10 to 12 minutes. Let cool slightly before serving. Serve with Cajun Sausage Gravy, jam, or honey.

HOMEMADE BUTTER

MAKES 1½ CUPS

Butter is what I do! I couldn't have a cookbook without giving y'all my butter recipe.

4 cups heavy whipping cream

1 tablespoon coarse sea salt, plus more for sprinkling

"One stick of butter, y'all!"

1 In the bowl of a stand mixer fitted with the whisk attachment, add cream. Place a kitchen towel over machine to contain splatters. Beat at medium speed until mixture begins to thicken, about 10 minutes. Add sea salt, and beat at medium speed until mixture separates, about 5 minutes.

2 Place a colander in a large bowl. Strain butter mixture, separating butter from buttermilk. Transfer buttermilk to a sealable container. Store in refrigerator for up to 1 week.

3 In a large bowl of ice water, place strained butter, and squeeze to remove excess buttermilk until water is clear, changing water often. Remove butter, and sprinkle with salt. Store butter, covered, in refrigerator for 1 to 2 weeks.

CHAPTER TWO

PARTY TIME

ONE THING YOU SHOULD KNOW IS THAT IN LOUISIANA, WE LOVE ANY EXCUSE TO HAVE A GOOD TIME. THE COMMUNITY WILL TURN OUT ANYTIME WE GET THE CHANCE. DON'T SHOW UP TO THE NEXT PARTY EMPTY-HANDED—BRING ONE OF MY FAVORITE PARTY STAPLES.

CRAWFISH QUESO DIP

MAKES 10 TO 12 SERVINGS

Need something to serve during the next football game? You can't keep this on the table—perfect dish to enjoy while watching the Saints win.

½ stick (¼ cup) unsalted butter

½ pound cooked crawfish tails

½ cup chopped yellow onion

½ cup chopped celery

½ cup chopped green bell pepper

3 teaspoons RTB Cajun Seasoning, divided

1 (1-pound) block Pepper Jack cheese, cut into 1-inch cubes

1 (1-pound) block white American cheese, cut into 1-inch cubes

1 (12-ounce) can evaporated milk

½ large jalapeño, chopped

1 cup shredded Cheddar cheese

Tortilla chips, to serve

1 Preheat an outdoor flattop griddle over medium heat. Add butter to one side of griddle. When butter melts, add crawfish, onion, celery, bell pepper, and 1½ teaspoons RTB Cajun Seasoning. Cook until vegetables are tender, 2 to 3 minutes, stirring occasionally.

2 Place a 10-inch cast-iron skillet on other side of griddle. Add Pepper Jack, American cheese, evaporated milk, jalapeño, and remaining 1½ teaspoons RTB Cajun Seasoning. Stir in crawfish mixture. Sprinkle Cheddar on top. Cover with foil, and cook until bubbly and melted, 20 to 25 minutes. Serve hot with tortilla chips.

RALPH'S TIP

I love cooking on my flattop griddle, but if you don't have one, that's OK. Take your cast-iron skillet and get to cooking inside! You can do everything on the stovetop, but if you want the cheese to get a little color, pop it in a 350° oven for a few minutes until it's nice and brown.

BOUDIN CHEESE BALL

MAKES 15 TO 20 SERVINGS

Boudin is a sausage that's popular here in Louisiana. It takes this traditional cheese ball to the next level. I dare you to try and take just one bite!

1 pound white boudin sausage, casings removed, crumbled

2 (8-ounce) packages cream cheese, softened

3½ cups shredded sharp Cheddar cheese

1 (1-ounce) package ranch dressing mix

2 cups chopped pecans

Buttery round crackers, to serve

Garnish: pecan halves

1 In a large skillet, cook boudin over medium heat until fully cooked, 6 to 8 minutes, stirring frequently. Drain excess grease, if any.

2 In a large bowl, mix together cooked boudin, cream cheese, Cheddar, and ranch dressing mix. Form into 1 large ball or 2 smaller balls. Roll in chopped pecans to coat surface. Wrap tightly in plastic wrap, and refrigerate for at least 2 hours, or overnight, before serving with crackers. Garnish with pecan halves, if desired.

Cajun Buffalo Dip

MAKES 10 TO 12 SERVINGS

Pretzels are the not-so-secret ingredient in this dip. Stirred into the cheese and placed on top, there's a satisfying crunch in every delicious bite.

2 sticks (1 cup) unsalted butter, divided

3 boneless skinless chicken breasts, cut into 1-inch cubes

2 teaspoons RTB Cajun Seasoning, divided

2 teaspoons RTB Dubba-U Sauce

½ cup plus 1 teaspoon RTB Cajun Hot Sauce, divided

½ teaspoon ground black pepper

2 (8-ounce) packages cream cheese, softened

2 cups shredded Pepper Jack cheese

2 cups shredded Colby-Jack cheese blend

2 cups shredded part-skim mozzarella cheese

1½ cups coarsely crushed pretzels*, divided

½ cup ranch dressing

¼ cup sliced green onion

¼ cup sour cream

Corn chips, to serve

1 Preheat an outdoor flattop griddle over medium heat. Add 1 stick (½ cup) butter to one side of griddle. When butter melts, add chicken, 1 teaspoon RTB Cajun Seasoning, RTB Dubba-U Sauce, 1 teaspoon RTB Cajun Hot Sauce, and pepper. Cook until chicken is cooked through, about 10 to 12 minutes, stirring occasionally.

2 While chicken cooks, place a 12-inch cast-iron skillet on other side of griddle. Add remaining 1 stick (½ cup) butter. When butter melts, add cream cheese, Pepper Jack, Colby-Jack, mozzarella, ½ cup pretzels, and remaining ½ cup RTB Cajun Hot Sauce, stirring until smooth.

3 Stir cooked chicken, ranch dressing, green onion, sour cream, and remaining 1 teaspoon RTB Cajun Seasoning into cheese mixture. Cook until hot and bubbly, about 20 minutes, stirring occasionally. Top with remaining 1 cup pretzels. Serve hot with corn chips.

I use Zapp's Sinfully-Seasoned Pretzel Stix Voodoo. They're a game changer.

Louisiana Hot Crab Dip

MAKES 6 TO 8 SERVINGS

I like this best hot out the oven with some crackers, but even right out of the fridge, this is full of flavor and great for any party.

½ pound jumbo lump crabmeat, picked free of shell

1 (8-ounce) package cream cheese, softened

½ cup mayonnaise

¼ cup freshly grated Parmesan cheese

3 tablespoons minced green onion

2 tablespoons fresh lemon juice

2 large cloves garlic, minced

2 teaspoons RTB Dubba-U Sauce

1 teaspoon RTB Cajun Hot Sauce

½ teaspoon RTB Cajun Seasoning

Buttery round crackers, to serve

1 Preheat oven to 325°.

2 In a large bowl, gently stir together crab, cream cheese, mayonnaise, Parmesan, green onion, lemon juice, garlic, RTB Dubba-U Sauce, RTB Cajun Hot Sauce, and RTB Cajun Seasoning until thoroughly mixed. Adjust seasonings to taste. Spoon into a 2-quart baking dish.

3 Bake until lightly golden on top, 35 to 40 minutes. Serve hot with crackers.

RALPH'S TIP

This is a great dip for your next tailgate. I like to make it the night before. Then, 40 minutes before the Saints kick off, I pop it in the oven and let it get nice and hot. As the game starts, the dip will be ready for friends and family to dig in.

FRIED GREEN TOMATOES

MAKES 4 SERVINGS

**It's not summer until I've had this Southern staple. Top them with
salt and see how fast your family eats them up.**

Vegetable oil, for frying

1 cup whole buttermilk

**3 teaspoons RTB Cajun Seasoning,
  divided**

1 cup fine yellow cornmeal

½ cup all-purpose flour

**1 teaspoon kosher salt,
  plus more to taste**

4 medium green tomatoes, sliced

1 In a large skillet, pour oil to fill halfway, and heat over medium-high heat until a deep-fry thermometer registers 350°.

2 In a small bowl, whisk together buttermilk and 1½ teaspoons RTB Cajun Seasoning. In a separate bowl, combine cornmeal, flour, salt, and remaining 1½ teaspoons RTB Cajun Seasoning. Dip tomato slices in buttermilk mixture, letting excess drip off; dredge in cornmeal mixture until well coated.

3 Fry coated tomato slices in batches until golden brown, about 2 minutes per side. Remove from oil, and let drain on paper towels. Sprinkle top with salt to taste. Serve hot.

BOUDIN DIP

MAKES 4 CUPS

A lot of people eat dip with chips, but you got to try this with some homemade Garlic Bread. It takes this over the top.

1 (8-ounce) package cream cheese, softened

1 (8-ounce) container sour cream, room temperature

1 pound white boudin sausage, casings removed, crumbled

1½ cups shredded Cheddar cheese, divided

¼ cup chopped green onion

2 teaspoons RTB Cajun Seasoning

Garlic Bread (recipe follows), to serve

Garnish: sliced green onion

1 Preheat oven to 350°.

2 In a large bowl, combine cream cheese and sour cream; stir in boudin, 1 cup Cheddar, and chopped green onion. Spoon into a 2-quart baking dish. Season with RTB Cajun Seasoning. Sprinkle with remaining ½ cup Cheddar.

3 Bake until bubbly, about 30 minutes. Serve hot with Garlic Bread. Garnish with sliced green onion, if desired.

GARLIC BREAD

MAKES 20 SLICES

1 (12-ounce) loaf French bread, cut into 1-inch slices

⅓ cup olive oil

½ teaspoon garlic powder

½ cup freshly grated Parmesan cheese

1 Preheat oven to 400°. Line a baking sheet with parchment paper.

2 Place bread on prepared pan. Brush slices with oil. Sprinkle with garlic powder. Top with cheese.

3 Bake until golden brown, 4 to 5 minutes.

Crawfish, Spinach, and Artichoke Dip

MAKES 8 SERVINGS

**My Cajun twist on the classic spinach and artichoke dip is full of flavor—and crawfish!
Everyone loves it, and they always ask me to make it when we're having a cookout.**

1 stick (½ cup) unsalted butter

1 cup chopped yellow onion

1 cup chopped celery

1 cup chopped red bell pepper

1 pound cooked crawfish tails

2 cups heavy whipping cream

2 cups shredded Colby-Jack
  cheese blend, divided

1½ cups shredded Parmesan cheese,
  divided

1 (8-ounce) package cream cheese,
  softened

1 tablespoon RTB Cajun Seasoning

1 teaspoon garlic powder

½ teaspoon ground black pepper

16 ounces frozen spinach,
  thawed and drained

1 (14-ounce) can artichoke hearts,
  drained and chopped

Corn chips, to serve

1 Preheat an outdoor flattop griddle over medium heat. Add butter to one side of griddle. When butter melts, add onion, celery, and bell pepper. Add crawfish; cook until vegetables are tender, about 5 minutes, stirring occasionally.

2 Place a 12-inch cast-iron skillet on other side of griddle. Add cream, 1 cup Colby-Jack, 1 cup Parmesan, cream cheese, RTB Cajun Seasoning, garlic powder, and pepper. Stir until smooth. Add spinach, artichoke, and crawfish mixture, stirring until combined. Top with remaining 1 cup Colby-Jack and remaining ½ cup Parmesan. Cook until cheese melts, about 8 minutes. Serve hot with corn chips.

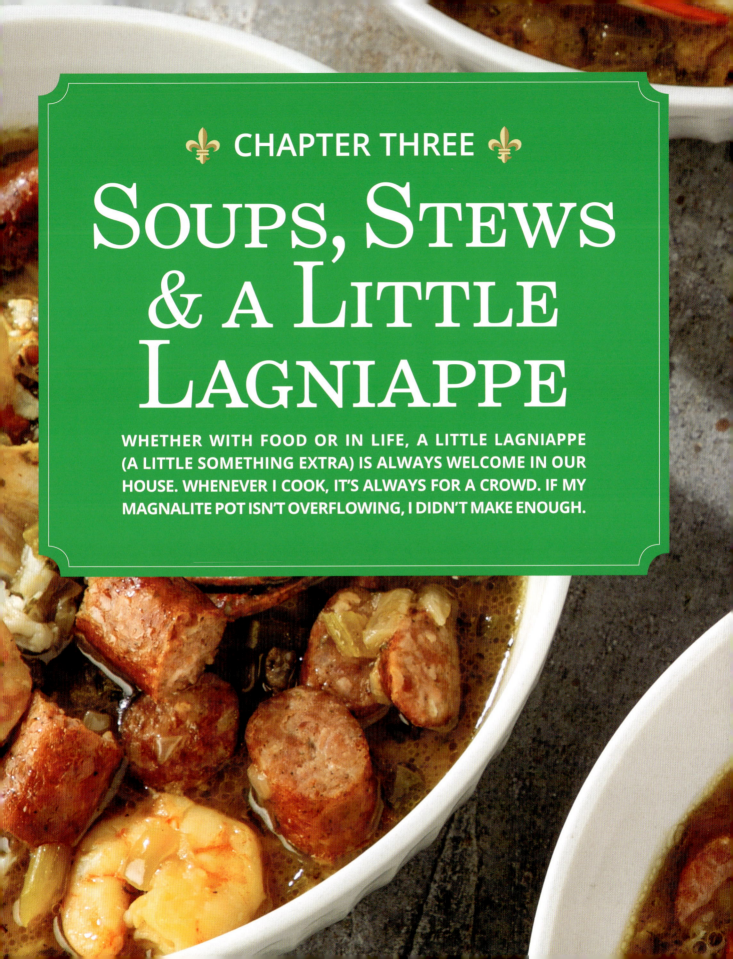

CHAPTER THREE

Soups, Stews & a Little Lagniappe

WHETHER WITH FOOD OR IN LIFE, A LITTLE LAGNIAPPE (A LITTLE SOMETHING EXTRA) IS ALWAYS WELCOME IN OUR HOUSE. WHENEVER I COOK, IT'S ALWAYS FOR A CROWD. IF MY MAGNALITE POT ISN'T OVERFLOWING, I DIDN'T MAKE ENOUGH.

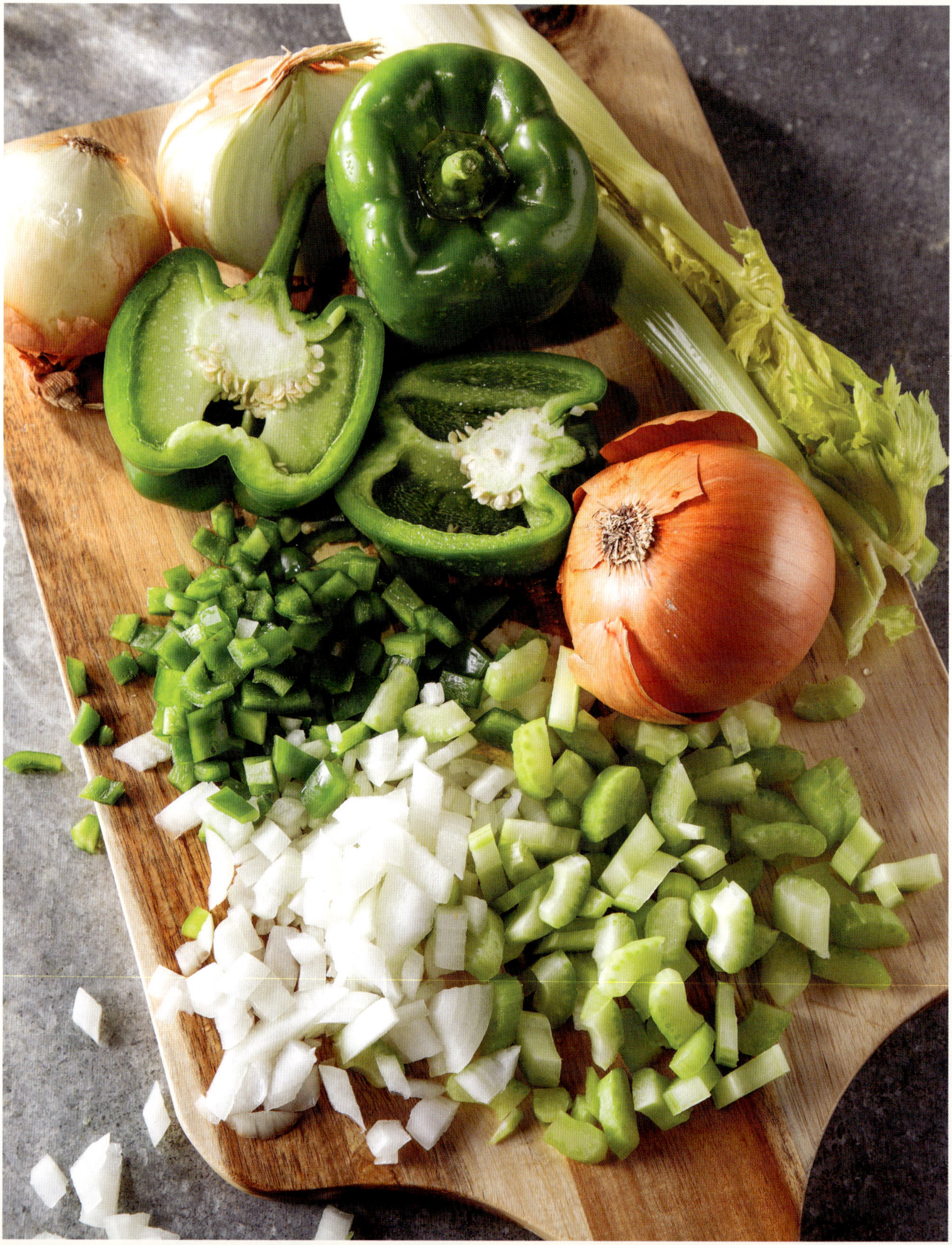

Holy Trinity

In New Orleans, our culture is closely tied with food. Almost every event, celebration, and belief is organized around what everyone will be eating. In my family, food is the tie that binds us together. Our history is deeply ingrained in the kitchen and around the dinner table as my mother and grandmother worked to feed our family.

One of the cornerstones of New Orleans cooking, which you'll find throughout this book, is known as the holy trinity: onion, celery, and bell pepper. Usually, the trinity is two parts onion, one part celery, and one part green bell pepper. From gumbo to crawfish étouffée, all the best dishes start with the holy trinity. In my cooking, you usually won't find the trinity without the pope (garlic)! Just be careful to wait until the trinity cooks down some before adding the pope or it'll burn. ⚜

Cajun Chili

MAKES 5 TO 6 SERVINGS

We don't get a lot of cold nights in Louisiana, but when we do, my family loves to make a big pot of our favorite chili. We eat ours with a little cheese and green onion on top!

2 tablespoons vegetable oil

2 stalks celery, diced

1 medium sweet onion, diced

1 medium green bell pepper, diced

1 tablespoon minced garlic

1½ pounds ground beef

2 (10-ounce) cans chunky
   tomato sauce

2 tablespoons chili powder

1 tablespoon RTB Cajun Seasoning

2 teaspoons kosher salt

1 (15.5-ounce) can red kidney
   beans, rinsed and drained

RTB Cajun Hot Sauce, to taste

Garnish: shredded Cheddar cheese,
   chopped green onion

1 In a 6-quart stockpot, heat oil over medium-high heat. Add celery, sweet onion, and bell pepper, and cook until soft, stirring occasionally. Stir in garlic. Push vegetables to the side, and add beef. Cook for 3 to 5 minutes, crumbling with a wooden spoon. Stir in tomato sauce, chili powder, RTB Cajun Seasoning, and salt, and cook until meat is cooked through, stirring frequently. (This will create a rich and thick sauce for the chili.) Add beans, and stir well. Simmer, uncovered, over medium-low heat for 30 to 45 minutes, stirring occasionally to prevent scorching or burning. Add RTB Cajun Hot Sauce to taste. Serve hot, and garnish each serving with cheese and green onion, if desired.

CAJUN POTATO AND SAUSAGE SOUP

MAKES 8 TO 10 SERVINGS

Smoked sausage is a staple in New Orleans cooking. You'll see it in a lot of my dishes. It gives everything a ton of flavor.

6 slices bacon, chopped

½ stick (¼ cup) unsalted butter

1 pound sausage (smoked sausage or sausage of your choice), sliced

4 cloves garlic, minced

3 stalks celery, diced

1 medium yellow onion, diced

5 cups diced peeled russet potatoes

6 cups chicken or vegetable broth

2 tablespoons onion powder

2 tablespoons RTB Cajun Seasoning

1½ teaspoons ground white pepper

1 teaspoon smoked paprika

½ teaspoon cayenne pepper (optional)

Kosher salt and ground black pepper, to taste

2 cups heavy whipping cream

Garnish: chopped green onion, chopped fresh parsley

1 In a Magnalite pot, cook bacon over medium heat until crispy, stirring occasionally. Remove bacon, and let drain on paper towels, reserving drippings in pot.

2 In same pot over medium heat, add butter. When butter melts, add sausage, and cook until browned, stirring occasionally. Remove sausage, and let drain on paper towels with bacon.

3 In same pot, add garlic, celery, and onion, and cook over medium heat until vegetables are softened, stirring occasionally. Add potatoes, and stir to combine. Pour in broth, and add onion powder, RTB Cajun Seasoning, white pepper, paprika, cayenne pepper (if using), and salt and black pepper to taste. Stir well. Bring soup to a boil. Reduce heat to low, cover, and simmer until potatoes are tender, 15 to 20 minutes. Stir in cooked bacon and sausage. Add cream; stir and let simmer for 5 to 10 minutes. Taste and adjust seasonings if needed. Serve hot, and garnish with green onion and parsley, if desired.

Swole's Sausage Connection has the best sausage, and they make it right here in Louisiana! I love to use their smoked sausage in my recipes any chance I can get.

FRIED OKRA

MAKES 8 TO 10 SERVINGS

There's a reason fried okra is nicknamed "Southern popcorn." You won't be able to stop eating it!

Vegetable oil, for frying

2 pounds fresh okra, trimmed and sliced crosswise ½ inch thick

2 cups whole buttermilk

2 cups fine yellow cornmeal

1 cup all-purpose flour

1 tablespoon RTB Cajun Seasoning

3 teaspoons kosher salt, divided

1½ teaspoons ground black pepper

½ teaspoon cayenne pepper (optional)

1 In a deep skillet or frying pan, pour oil to a depth of 2 inches, and heat over medium-high heat until a deep-fry thermometer registers 350°.

2 In a large bowl, add okra and buttermilk, and let stand for 15 to 30 minutes. (This will help reduce the slime in the okra.)

3 In another large bowl, mix together cornmeal, flour, RTB Cajun Seasoning, 1½ teaspoons salt, black pepper, and cayenne pepper (if using). Working in batches, remove okra from buttermilk, letting excess drip off, and dredge in cornmeal mixture, pressing mixture onto okra to ensure it sticks.

4 Fry okra in batches until golden brown and crispy, 3 to 4 minutes, turning occasionally. (Do not overcrowd pan.) Remove using a slotted spoon, and let drain on paper towels. Sprinkle with remaining 1½ teaspoons salt. Let cool slightly before serving.

HUSH PUPPIES

MAKES 32

Crispy on the outside and soft on the inside, these are full of flavor.
They're the perfect side to your favorite fried seafood.

Vegetable oil, for frying

1 cup fine yellow cornmeal

½ cup all-purpose flour

1 teaspoon baking powder

½ teaspoon kosher salt

½ cup finely chopped yellow onion

½ cup whole buttermilk

1 large egg, beaten

1 In a cast-iron skillet or a heavy-bottomed pan, pour oil to a depth of 1½ inches, and heat over medium heat until a deep-fry thermometer registers 350°.

2 In a large bowl, combine cornmeal, flour, baking powder, and salt. Add onion, buttermilk, and egg, and mix until just combined.

3 Drop spoonfuls of batter into hot oil, and fry until golden brown, turning as needed. Using a slotted spoon, remove and let drain on paper towels. Let cool slightly before serving.

CHICKEN AND DUMPLINGS

MAKES 6 TO 8 SERVINGS

This hearty chicken soup is topped with spoonfuls of savory dumplings. It's an easy meal that is all about comfort and flavor.

1 whole chicken, neck and giblets removed, cut into pieces

1 teaspoon kosher salt, divided

½ teaspoon ground black pepper, plus more to serve

2 tablespoons vegetable oil

3 medium carrots, peeled and sliced

3 celery stalks, sliced

1 medium yellow onion, finely chopped

4 cups chicken broth

2 tablespoons RTB Cajun Seasoning

1½ teaspoons onion powder

1½ teaspoons garlic powder

1 teaspoon dried thyme

2 cups all-purpose flour

1 cup whole milk

1 tablespoon baking powder

1 Season chicken pieces with ½ teaspoon salt and pepper.

2 In a large pot, heat oil over medium heat. Add chicken, and cook until lightly browned, about 5 minutes per side. Add carrots, celery, and onion. Cook until vegetables are softened, stirring occasionally. Pour in chicken broth, RTB Cajun Seasoning, onion powder, garlic powder, and thyme. Bring to a simmer; reduce heat, cover, and cook for about 30 minutes. Remove chicken from broth, and let cool slightly. Remove chicken from bone, and discard bones. Shred the chicken, and add back to broth.

3 In a bowl, whisk together flour, milk, baking powder, and remaining ½ teaspoon salt until a soft dough forms. Drop spoonfuls of dough into simmering broth. Cover and cook until dumplings are cooked through, 15 to 20 minutes. Serve hot with a sprinkle of pepper.

Roux

MAKES ABOUT 2 CUPS

This is a Cajun and Creole staple for many stews, gumbos, soups, and more. Part fat, part flour, this simple combo will get your gumbos and stews nice and thick and give them a great flavor. Do your roux low and slow, and it'll be perfect every time.

1¼ cups all-purpose flour

1¼ cups vegetable oil

1 In a Dutch oven, combine flour and vegetable oil, and cook over medium heat for 8 to 10 minutes, stirring constantly with a flat-edged wooden spoon.

2 Reduce heat to medium-low to avoid burning. Cook until mixture goes from a pale color to a golden color and then to a rich chocolate-brown color and has a nutty scent, 15 to 30 minutes (see note), stirring constantly. Remove from heat, and let cool slightly.

NOTE: *Patience is key. It takes time to develop a dark roux, and rushing can result in a burnt taste. The roux will go through several color stages. In the beginning, it will be pale and then turn golden, and finally, it will darken to a rich chocolate-brown color. This process can take anywhere from 15 to 30 minutes, or more depending on the heat level. The roux will have a nutty, almost burnt smell as it darkens. Be attentive to the scent, as it can help you gauge the roux's progress. Once it's the desired color, immediately remove from heat. Keep in mind that the roux will continue to cook a bit even after being removed from the heat due to residual heat in the pot.*

Blond Roux

MAKES ABOUT 2 CUPS

2½ sticks (1¼ cups) unsalted butter

1¼ cups all-purpose flour

1 In a Dutch oven over medium heat, add butter. When butter melts, add flour, and cook for 8 to 10 minutes, stirring constantly with a flat-edged wooden spoon.

2 Reduce heat to medium-low to avoid burning. Cook until mixture goes from a pale color to a golden color, 15 to 20 minutes, stirring constantly. Remove from heat, and let cool slightly before using.

RALPH'S TIPS

- Use a heavy-bottomed, preferably cast-iron, pot. The material and weight of the pot help distribute heat evenly, preventing hot spots that can burn the roux.
- Stirring is crucial to prevent burning and ensure even browning. Don't stop stirring!
- The ratio of flour to fat is typically 1:1, but you can adjust it slightly based on your preference for a thicker or thinner roux.

Peanut Butter-Colored Roux

OKRA CREOLE

MAKES 6 SERVINGS

Don't like okra? It's only because you've never had it cooked right. Bacon, tomatoes, and seasoning add a ton of flavor to this dish. Everyone will love it.

3 slices bacon

1 (16-ounce) package frozen sliced okra

1 (14.5-ounce) can chopped tomatoes

1 cup frozen corn kernels

½ cup water

1 tablespoon onion powder

1 teaspoon RTB Cajun Seasoning

¼ teaspoon ground black pepper

Hot cooked white rice, to serve

1 In a large Dutch oven, cook bacon over medium-high heat until crisp, turning halfway through cooking. Remove bacon, and let drain on paper towels, reserving drippings in pot. Crumble bacon, and set aside.

2 In same pot, add okra, tomatoes, corn, ½ cup water, onion powder, RTB Cajun Seasoning, and pepper; cook over medium-high heat for 5 minutes, stirring occasionally. Reduce heat to low, cover, and simmer until vegetables are tender, about 15 minutes. Top with crumbled bacon. Serve hot over rice.

SHRIMP STEW

MAKES 10 TO 12 SERVINGS

Between the roux and homemade stock, people think shrimp stew is too hard to make from scratch. I made this one easy to follow. You'll have a delicious meal in no time.

2 cups peanut butter-colored Roux (recipe on page 60)

1½ cups chopped yellow onion

1½ cups chopped celery

1½ cups chopped green bell pepper

2 pounds smoked sausage, sliced

3 (32-ounce) containers chicken broth

3 tablespoons minced garlic

8 medium-size Yukon gold potatoes, peeled and cut into 1½-inch chunks

3 tablespoons RTB Dubba-U Sauce

2 tablespoons RTB Cajun Seasoning

2 tablespoons onion powder

2 teaspoons kosher salt

2 teaspoons ground black pepper

2 pounds peeled and deveined medium fresh shrimp

Hot cooked white rice, to serve

1 In a large cast-iron Dutch oven, add Roux, onion, celery, and bell pepper, and cook over medium-low heat until vegetables are tender, 5 to 7 minutes, stirring occasionally. Add sausage, and cook until browned, about 8 minutes, stirring occasionally. Slowly stir in chicken broth and garlic. Add potatoes, RTB Dubba-U Sauce, RTB Cajun Seasoning, onion powder, salt, and pepper. Bring to a gentle boil over medium-high heat, stirring occasionally. Reduce heat to medium-low; cook until potatoes are almost tender, about 30 minutes, stirring occasionally.

2 Add shrimp to stew; cook until shrimp are pink and firm, about 5 minutes, stirring occasionally. Taste and adjust seasonings if needed. Serve hot over rice.

Seafood Gumbo

MAKES 6 TO 8 SERVINGS

It takes a few hours to make this dish, but it's worth the wait with all the sausage, crab, and shrimp.

1 cup peanut butter-colored Roux
  (recipe on page 60)

4 stalks celery, diced

1 medium yellow onion, diced

1 large green bell pepper, diced

3 pounds smoked sausage, sliced

2 (48-ounce) containers seafood broth

24 gumbo crabs

14 ounces lump crabmeat, picked
  free of shell

2 tablespoons RTB Dubba-U Sauce

1 tablespoon kosher salt

1 tablespoon garlic powder

1 tablespoon onion powder

1 tablespoon dried parsley

2 teaspoons RTB Cajun Seasoning

2 teaspoons ground black pepper

3 dried bay leaves

2 pounds peeled and deveined
  medium fresh shrimp

1 In a large Magnalite pot, add Roux, celery, onion, and bell pepper, and cook over medium-low heat until vegetables are tender, stirring occasionally.

2 While vegetables are cooking, in a medium skillet, cook sausage over medium heat until browned, about 8 minutes, stirring occasionally. Remove sausage, and let drain on paper towels.

3 Add browned sausage and seafood broth to vegetable mixture, stirring until well combined. Add gumbo crabs, crabmeat, RTB Dubba-U Sauce, salt, garlic powder, onion powder, parsley, RTB Cajun Seasoning, black pepper, and bay leaves, stirring to combine. Cover and cook for 2 hours, stirring occasionally.

4 Add shrimp to gumbo. Cover and cook for 30 minutes, stirring occasionally. Serve hot.

RALPH'S TIP

The key to a good gumbo is a good roux. Follow the recipe carefully and get it to that rich peanut butter color. (You can go a little darker if you want an even deeper flavor!) Getting your roux right takes 30 to 40 minutes of active cooking. Never walk away from a roux.

Corn and Crab Bisque

MAKES 10 SERVINGS

I love to make this in my Magnalite pot. You'll find them in most Louisiana kitchens. They're great when cooking for the whole family.

1 stick (½ cup) unsalted butter

1 cup chopped white onion

1 cup chopped celery

1 cup chopped green bell pepper

2 (14.75-ounce) cans creamed corn

1 (22.6-ounce) can cream of
   mushroom soup

2 (10-ounce) bags frozen corn kernels,
   thawed

4 cups half-and-half

3 cups chicken broth

1 cup chopped fresh parsley

¾ cup Blond Roux (recipe on page 60)

2 teaspoons RTB Cajun Seasoning

2 teaspoons garlic powder

2 teaspoons onion powder

1 teaspoon ground black pepper

2 pounds lump crabmeat, picked
   free of shell

¼ cup bottled minced garlic

½ teaspoon liquid crab boil

1 In a large Magnalite pot over medium heat, add butter. When butter melts, add onion, celery, and bell pepper. Cook until softened, 6 to 7 minutes, stirring frequently. Add creamed corn, soup, thawed corn, half-and-half, chicken broth, parsley, Blond Roux, RTB Cajun Seasoning, garlic powder, onion powder, and pepper, stirring to combine. Gently stir in crab, garlic, and crab boil. Cover and simmer for 30 minutes, stirring occasionally. Serve hot.

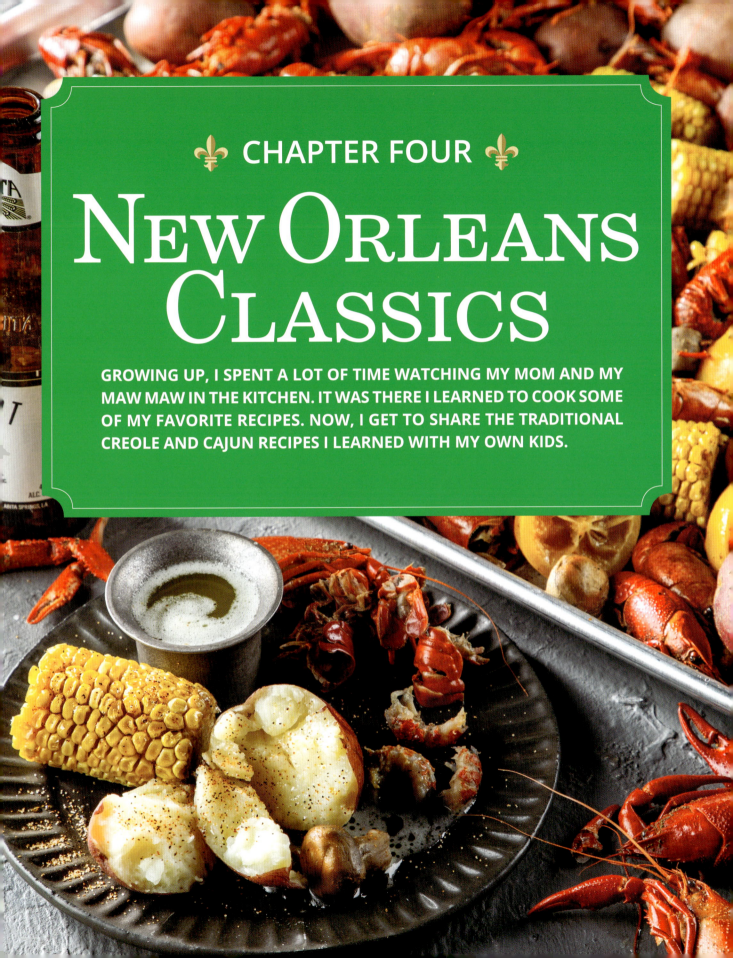

CHAPTER FOUR
⚜ ⚜

NEW ORLEANS CLASSICS

GROWING UP, I SPENT A LOT OF TIME WATCHING MY MOM AND MY MAW MAW IN THE KITCHEN. IT WAS THERE I LEARNED TO COOK SOME OF MY FAVORITE RECIPES. NOW, I GET TO SHARE THE TRADITIONAL CREOLE AND CAJUN RECIPES I LEARNED WITH MY OWN KIDS.

ALLIGATOR SAUCE PIQUANT

MAKES 6 SERVINGS

This traditional Louisiana recipe pairs tender alligator meat with a spicy tomato sauce. Served over white rice, this is some good stuff.

⅓ cup peanut butter-colored Roux (recipe on page 60)

4 cloves garlic, minced

2 stalks celery, finely chopped

1 large yellow onion, finely chopped

1 medium green bell pepper, finely chopped

1 (14-ounce) can crushed tomatoes

2 cups beef broth

1 cup water

¼ cup RTB Dubba-U Sauce

2 tablespoons tomato paste

2 dried bay leaves

1 tablespoon RTB Cajun Seasoning

1 teaspoon dried thyme

1 teaspoon paprika

Kosher salt and ground black pepper, to taste

1½ pounds boneless alligator meat, cut into bite-size pieces

Hot cooked white rice, to serve

1 In a large heavy-bottomed pot, add Roux, garlic, celery, onion, and bell pepper, and cook over medium-low heat until vegetables are softened, 3 to 4 minutes, stirring frequently. Stir in crushed tomatoes, beef broth, 1 cup water, RTB Dubba-U Sauce, tomato paste, bay leaves, RTB Cajun Seasoning, thyme, paprika, and salt and pepper to taste. Bring to a simmer over medium heat. Add alligator meat. Reduce heat to low; cover and simmer until alligator is tender, 1 to 1½ hours, stirring occasionally. Taste and adjust seasonings if needed. Once alligator is tender and flavors have blended, discard bay leaves. Serve hot over rice.

CRAWFISH ÉTOUFFÉE

MAKES 6 SERVINGS

In this recipe, meaty crawfish tails are served in a rich, buttery sauce over rice. If you can't find crawfish near you, you can use shrimp.

¼ cup Blond Roux (recipe on page 60)

3 cloves garlic, minced

2 stalks celery, chopped

1 medium yellow onion, chopped

1 medium green bell pepper, chopped

2 cups chicken broth

1 (8-ounce) can tomato sauce

2 tablespoons RTB Cajun Seasoning

1½ teaspoons garlic powder

1½ teaspoons onion powder

½ teaspoon cayenne pepper (optional)

Kosher salt and ground black pepper, to taste

1 pound fresh crawfish tail meat

Hot cooked white rice, to serve

Garnish: chopped fresh parsley, sliced green onion

1 In a large Magnalite pot, add Blond Roux, garlic, celery, yellow onion, and bell pepper, and cook over medium-low heat until vegetables are softened, 3 to 4 minutes, stirring frequently. Slowly add chicken broth, and stir until smooth. Add tomato sauce, and continue stirring. Add RTB Cajun Seasoning, garlic powder, onion powder, cayenne pepper (if using), and salt and black pepper to taste; stir until well combined. Reduce heat to low, and simmer until thickened, 15 to 20 minutes, stirring occasionally. Add crawfish, and simmer until cooked through, 3 to 5 minutes. Serve hot over rice. Garnish with parsley and green onion, if desired.

CRAWFISH BOIL

MAKES 15 SERVINGS

You can't get through April in Louisiana without at least one crawfish boil. Crawfish, sausage, potatoes, onions, and garlic—you can't beat it!

1 (30- to 35-pound) sack live fresh crawfish

1 (2-pound) package RTB Seafood Boil Seasoning

10 medium yellow onions, halved

1 (5-pound) bag red potatoes

10 heads garlic

10 lemons, halved

1 bunch celery, trimmed, stalks cut in half

1 cup fresh lemon juice

1 (1-pound) container whole white mushrooms

10 ears corn, halved

2 pounds smoked sausage, cut into 3-inch pieces

1 To clean crawfish, place in a large container (such as a cooler), and add water. Stir crawfish, and drain water. Repeat process until water remains clear. (This may take about three times.) Discard any dead crawfish. (They won't be moving.)

2 Place a large outdoor 60-quart pot with a crawfish basket on a heavy-duty outdoor burner. Fill halfway with water. Add RTB Seafood Boil Seasoning, onion, potatoes, garlic, lemons, celery, and lemon juice. Heat water to 200°. Cook for 10 minutes, stirring occasionally. Add crawfish. Cook for 2 minutes. Add mushrooms, corn, and sausage. Boil for 3 minutes. Turn off heat.

3 Using a garden hose, spray water around outside of pot, cooling mixture. Continue to stir while mixture cools to 160°. Let stand for 10 to 15 minutes, allowing crawfish to absorb seasoning. Drain, and discard onion and celery.

MINI CRAWFISH PIES

MAKES 8 TO 10 MINI PIES

I like to make these for people to enjoy on Sundays when we watch the Saints play. I can guarantee everyone is going to love them!

½ stick (¼ cup) unsalted butter

1 cup chopped yellow onion

½ cup chopped green bell pepper

¼ cup chopped celery

½ cup chopped canned tomatoes

1½ teaspoons kosher salt

½ teaspoon cayenne pepper

1 pound fresh crawfish tails

½ cup water

2 tablespoons all-purpose flour

¼ cup chopped green onion

¼ cup chopped fresh parsley

8 to 10 frozen mini piecrusts

1 In a large skillet, melt butter over medium heat. Add onion, bell pepper, and celery; cook until vegetables are soft and golden, 10 to 12 minutes, stirring occasionally. Add tomatoes, salt, and cayenne pepper; cook for about 5 minutes, stirring occasionally. Add crawfish tails, and cook for about 5 minutes, stirring occasionally.

2 In a small bowl, add ½ cup water and flour, stirring until flour dissolves. Stir flour mixture into crawfish mixture, and cook for 2 to 3 minutes, stirring until mixture thickens. Add green onion and parsley, stirring to combine. Remove from heat, and let cool for about 30 minutes.

3 Preheat oven to 375°.

4 Spoon crawfish mixture evenly into piecrusts. Place on a rimmed baking sheet.

5 Bake until edges of piecrusts are golden, about 45 minutes. Let cool for several minutes before serving.

RALPH'S TIP

You can make this as one big 9-inch pie. You can make the piecrust from scratch (see page 248), or you can use a 9-inch frozen deep-dish pie crust. I do both, depending on how much time I have!

CREOLE DIRTY RICE

MAKES 4 SERVINGS

The traditional way to make dirty rice is with chicken liver, but my version is made with ground beef. I prefer the flavor, and it guarantees my kids will eat it! But if you like the livers, you can add them in (see note).

½ pound ground beef or ground pork

1 cup finely chopped yellow onion

½ cup finely chopped celery

½ cup finely chopped green bell pepper

3 cloves garlic, minced

1 cup long-grain white rice

2 cups chicken broth

½ stick (¼ cup) unsalted butter

2 tablespoons RTB Dubba-U Sauce

1 tablespoon RTB Cajun Seasoning

½ teaspoon dried thyme

½ teaspoon paprika

¼ teaspoon cayenne pepper, or
   to taste

Kosher salt and ground black pepper,
   to taste

Garnish: chopped green onion,
   chopped fresh parsley

1 In a large skillet or Dutch oven, cook ground beef or pork over medium-high heat until browned, breaking it up with a spoon as it cooks. Add yellow onion, celery, and bell pepper. Cook until vegetables are tender, 5 to 6 minutes, stirring occasionally. Stir in garlic, and cook for 1 minute. Add rice, and stir to coat rice with meat mixture. Stir in chicken broth, butter, RTB Dubba-U Sauce, RTB Cajun Seasoning, thyme, paprika, cayenne pepper, and salt and black pepper to taste. Stir well to combine. Bring to a boil over high heat. Reduce heat to low, cover, and simmer until rice is cooked and has absorbed liquid, 18 to 20 minutes. Fluff rice with a fork. Taste and adjust seasonings if needed. Serve hot with green onion and parsley, if desired.

NOTE: *If you want to add puréed chicken livers, add in with ground meat.*

JAMBALAYA

MAKES 6 TO 8 SERVINGS

The difference between Creole and Cajun jambalaya is tomatoes. Sarah, my wife, loves it with tomatoes, so we make a lot of Creole jambalaya in our house.

½ pound boneless skinless chicken breasts, cut into 1-inch pieces

½ pound boneless skinless chicken thighs, cut into 1-inch pieces

3 tablespoons RTB Cajun Seasoning, divided

1½ teaspoons kosher salt, divided

1½ teaspoons garlic powder, divided

1½ teaspoons onion powder, divided

1½ teaspoons ground black pepper, divided

½ stick (¼ cup) unsalted butter

½ pound sliced andouille sausage or smoked sausage

2 stalks celery, chopped

1 medium yellow onion, chopped

1 medium green bell pepper, chopped

3 cloves garlic, minced

1 (14.5-ounce) can diced tomatoes

2 to 3 cups chicken broth, divided

1 cup parboiled or long-grain white rice

2 dried bay leaves

2 tablespoons RTB Dubba-U Sauce

1 to 2 tablespoons RTB Cajun Hot Sauce

½ pound peeled and deveined medium fresh shrimp

4 green onions, thinly sliced

1 In a large bowl, combine all chicken, 1½ tablespoons RTB Cajun Seasoning, ¾ teaspoon salt, ¾ teaspoon garlic powder, ¾ teaspoon onion powder, and ¾ teaspoon pepper.

2 In a large skillet, melt butter over medium-high heat. Add chicken, and cook until browned, 8 to 10 minutes per side. Add sausage, and cook until sausage begins to brown, about 3 minutes, stirring occasionally. Add celery, onion, and bell pepper, and cook for 3 to 4 minutes, stirring occasionally. Add garlic, and cook for 1 minute, stirring occasionally. Add tomatoes and 2 cups chicken broth. Add rice, stirring to combine. Stir in remaining 1½ tablespoons RTB Cajun Seasoning, remaining ¾ teaspoon salt, remaining ¾ teaspoon garlic powder, remaining ¾ teaspoon onion powder, and remaining ¾ teaspoon pepper. Add bay leaves, RTB Dubba-U Sauce, and RTB Cajun Hot Sauce, stirring to combine. Bring to a boil. Reduce heat to medium-low, cover, and simmer, stirring occasionally, for 15 minutes.

3 Add shrimp to jambalaya, cover, and simmer until rice is tender and liquid is gone, about 10 minutes. If liquid cooks out before the rice is cooked, add up to 1 cup remaining chicken broth as needed. Serve hot with green onion.

NOTE: *It is common for jambalaya to stick to the bottom of the skillet or pot as the liquid cooks out. Make sure to scrape the bottom when stirring.*

New Orleans Crab Cakes

MAKES 6

Rich, crispy, and loaded with crabmeat, these pan-fried crab cakes are full of flavor. My trick is to squeeze some fresh lemon juice on them right before eating for the perfect bite.

½ medium yellow onion, minced

2 large eggs

2 tablespoons RTB Cajun Seasoning

2 tablespoons mayonnaise

1 tablespoon Creole mustard

1 pound crabmeat or claw meat, picked free of shell and drained

2 cups dried bread crumbs, divided

Vegetable oil, for frying

Fresh lemon juice and tartar sauce, to serve

1 In a large bowl, add onion, eggs, RTB Cajun Seasoning, mayonnaise, and mustard; mix until smooth. Gently fold in crab. (Do not overmix.) Slowly add up to 1 cup bread crumbs until you reach your desired consistency. (If it's still too wet to shape, fold in more bread crumbs.) Evenly divide and shape mixture into 6 (1-inch-thick) hockey puck-shaped patties.

2 In a shallow dish, add remaining 1 cup bread crumbs. Dredge each patty in bread crumbs until coated on all sides.

3 In a large cast-iron skillet, pour oil to a depth of ¼ inch, and heat over medium-high heat until a deep-fry thermometer registers 350°. Fry crab cakes in batches until golden brown, 2 to 4 minutes per side. Remove from skillet, and let drain on paper towels. Squeeze lemon juice over each crab cake, and serve hot with tartar sauce.

My internet friends will recognize this setup any day! This is where I film most of my cooking videos. Over the years, we've added onto the backyard kitchen with some fun new toys, but I always love cooking on my recteq griddle. Sarah, my wife, helps film my videos, and my kids like to make appearances here and there. We've made a lot of great memories as a family in this backyard.

MIRLITON CASSEROLE

MAKES 8 SERVINGS

Mirlitons are green, pear-shaped squash that are popular here in Louisiana, especially around the holidays. This casserole is a family favorite.

6 medium mirlitons

½ stick (¼ cup) unsalted butter, softened

6 cloves garlic, minced

4 green onions, thinly sliced

2 stalks celery, finely diced

1 medium yellow onion, finely chopped

1 medium tomato, seeded and diced

1 cup roughly chopped fresh mushrooms

½ medium green bell pepper, finely diced

½ medium red bell pepper, finely diced

2 pounds peeled and deveined large fresh shrimp, chopped

1 pound Polish sausage, diced

¼ cup minced fresh parsley

1 teaspoon kosher salt

½ teaspoon chopped fresh thyme

½ teaspoon chopped fresh rosemary

½ teaspoon crushed red pepper

½ teaspoon ground black pepper

4 cups French Bread Crumbs (recipe follows)

1 large egg, well beaten

½ cup cornflakes

¼ stick (2 tablespoons) unsalted butter, melted

½ cup shredded Parmesan cheese

---

1 In a large pot, add mirlitons and lightly salted water to cover; bring to a boil over high heat, and cook until an ice pick will pierce them all the way through without using excessive pressure. Drain, and let cool.

2 In a 5-quart Dutch oven, melt softened butter over medium heat. Add garlic, green onion, celery, yellow onion, tomato, mushrooms, and bell peppers; cook until tender, about 5 minutes, stirring occasionally.

3 Slice cooked mirlitons in half lengthwise, discarding center seedpods. Using a paring knife, carefully peel outer skin away from pulp. Once skin is removed, dice pulp into small pieces, and set aside.

4 Preheat oven to 325°.

5 In same Dutch oven, add shrimp and sausage, and cook over high heat until shrimp are pink and firm and sausage is browned slightly around edges, 2 to 4 minutes, stirring occasionally. Add mirliton pulp, and reduce heat to medium-high. Cook until a chunky paste forms (it may turn slightly watery, but don't worry about it), 10 to 15 minutes, stirring constantly. Fold in parsley, salt, thyme, rosemary, crushed red pepper, and black pepper. Add French Bread Crumbs, 1 cup at a time, stirring until a dry paste that sticks to the spoon forms. (See note.) Stir in egg. Transfer mixture to a cast-iron Dutch oven.

6 In a small bowl, stir together cornflakes and melted butter until cornflakes are well coated and crumbly. Sprinkle on top of casserole.

7 Bake, uncovered, until topping turns a toasty brown, 25 to 30 minutes. Sprinkle Parmesan on top. Serve hot.

NOTE: *If the mixture is too wet, it will run during the baking process. If, on the other hand, your stuffing mix turns out too dry, simply add chicken broth, 1 tablespoon at a time, until the mixture is moistened to your liking.*

French Bread Crumbs
MAKES 2 CUPS

1 loaf French bread, cut into 1-inch cubes

Olive oil, kosher salt, garlic powder, and onion powder, to taste

1 Preheat oven to 350°. Line a rimmed baking sheet with parchment paper.

2 In a large bowl, add bread cubes and olive oil, salt, garlic powder, and onion powder to taste, tossing to coat. Spread coated bread cubes in an even layer on prepared pan.

3 Bake until bread begins to turn golden brown, 3 to 5 minutes. Toss and bake until bread is crispy to the touch, 3 to 5 minutes more. Let cool completely.

4 In the work bowl of a food processer, pulse toasted bread cubes on high until crumbs form, about 1 minute.

RALPH'S TIPS

• For extra flavor, add in some cubed smoked ham or pickled pork.
• If you like a creamier and thicker texture, you can use the back of a spoon to mash some of the beans against the side of the pot.

New Orleans Red Beans & Rice

MAKES 8 SERVINGS

There are a lot of different recipes for red beans out there, but this is a true version of what you'd actually get in New Orleans. And you always cook red beans on Monday!

1 pound dried red kidney beans

½ stick (¼ cup) unsalted butter

2 stalks celery, chopped

1 medium yellow onion, chopped

1 medium green bell pepper, chopped

1 pound andouille sausage or smoked sausage, sliced

3 cloves garlic, minced

4 cups chicken broth

2 cups water, plus more as needed

2 dried bay leaves

1 tablespoon garlic powder

1 tablespoon onion powder

1 tablespoon dried parsley

1½ teaspoons dried oregano

1½ teaspoons dried thyme

½ teaspoon cayenne pepper

Kosher salt and ground black pepper, to taste

Hot cooked white rice, to serve

Garnish: sliced green onion

1 Rinse kidney beans thoroughly and remove any debris. In a large bowl or pot, add rinsed beans and water to cover; let soak overnight. (If you're in a hurry, you can use the quick-soak method; see note.)

2 In a large Magnalite pot, melt butter over medium heat. Add celery, yellow onion, and bell pepper. Cook over medium-high heat until softened, about 5 minutes, stirring occasionally. Add sausage, and cook until browned, about 5 minutes, stirring occasionally. Stir in garlic, and cook for 1 minute.

3 Drain beans, and add to vegetable mixture. Add chicken broth and 2 cups water, making sure beans are covered with liquid. Stir in bay leaves, garlic powder, onion powder, parsley, oregano, thyme, cayenne pepper, and salt and black pepper to taste, and bring to a boil.

4 Reduce heat to low, cover, and simmer until beans are tender, 2 to 3 hours, stirring occasionally. (Add more water if needed to keep beans covered.) Discard bay leaves. Serve hot over rice. Garnish with green onion, if desired.

NOTE: *For the quick-soak method, in a large pot, add kidney beans and water to cover, and bring to a boil. Remove from heat, and let soak for 1 hour before draining.*

New Orleans Muffuletta

MAKES 1

I love this classic sandwich full of deli meat, mozzarella, and olive salad (the most important part!). In New Orleans, you can get it half, whole, or in quarters. We like to serve it in quarters at Christmas.

1 (9- to 10-inch) loaf muffuletta bread or round Italian bread, halved horizontally

1½ cups olive salad, oil drained and reserved

¼ pound deli ham (4 to 6 slices)

¼ pound salami (6 to 8 slices)

¼ pound mortadella (4 to 6 slices)

⅛ pound sliced mozzarella (3 to 4 thin slices)

⅛ pound sliced provolone (3 to 4 thin slices)

1 Brush cut sides of bread with reserved oil from olive salad. (Extra-virgin olive oil can be used as well.)

2 On bottom half of bread, place ham, salami, mortadella, mozzarella, and provolone. Add olive salad, starting in center and gently spreading across. Cover with top half of bread. Cut into 4 to 6 wedges.

NOTE: *The beginning and end to a great muffuletta is using a quality Italian-style olive salad. My go-to is Boscoli Family Italian Olive Salad.*

RALPH'S TIP

Muffulettas can be served cold or hot. To serve hot, preheat oven to 350°. Prepare sandwich through step 2 before slicing. Place on a baking sheet. Bake for about 5 minutes. Cut into 4 to 6 wedges.

YAKA MEIN

MAKES 6 TO 8 SERVINGS

This dish is famous among locals, but outside of New Orleans, not many people know about this Creole-Asian noodle soup. It's a must-have after a night out!

1 stick (½ cup) unsalted butter

2½ pounds beef chuck roast, cut into 1-inch cubes

2 tablespoons RTB Dubba-U Sauce

1 tablespoon onion powder

1 tablespoon garlic powder

1 tablespoon RTB Cajun Seasoning

1 teaspoon ground black pepper

Kosher salt, to taste

3 (32-ounce) containers beef broth

2 tablespoons soy sauce

1 tablespoon dried parsley

2 pounds long macaroni (see note), cooked according to package directions

Halved hard-boiled eggs, RTB Cajun Hot Sauce, and sliced green onion, to serve

1 In a large Magnalite pot, melt butter over medium-high heat. Add beef, RTB Dubba-U Sauce, onion powder, garlic powder, RTB Cajun Seasoning, pepper, and salt to taste. Cook until beef is browned, 8 to 10 minutes, stirring occasionally. Add beef broth, soy sauce, and parsley, stirring to combine. Taste and adjust seasonings if needed. Bring to a gentle boil; reduce heat to medium-low. Cover and simmer until beef is very tender, about 2 hours, stirring occasionally.

2 Place long macaroni into individual serving bowls, and top with beef and broth. Serve with eggs, RTB Cajun Hot Sauce, and green onion.

NOTE: *If you can't find long macaroni near you, you can use bucatini.*

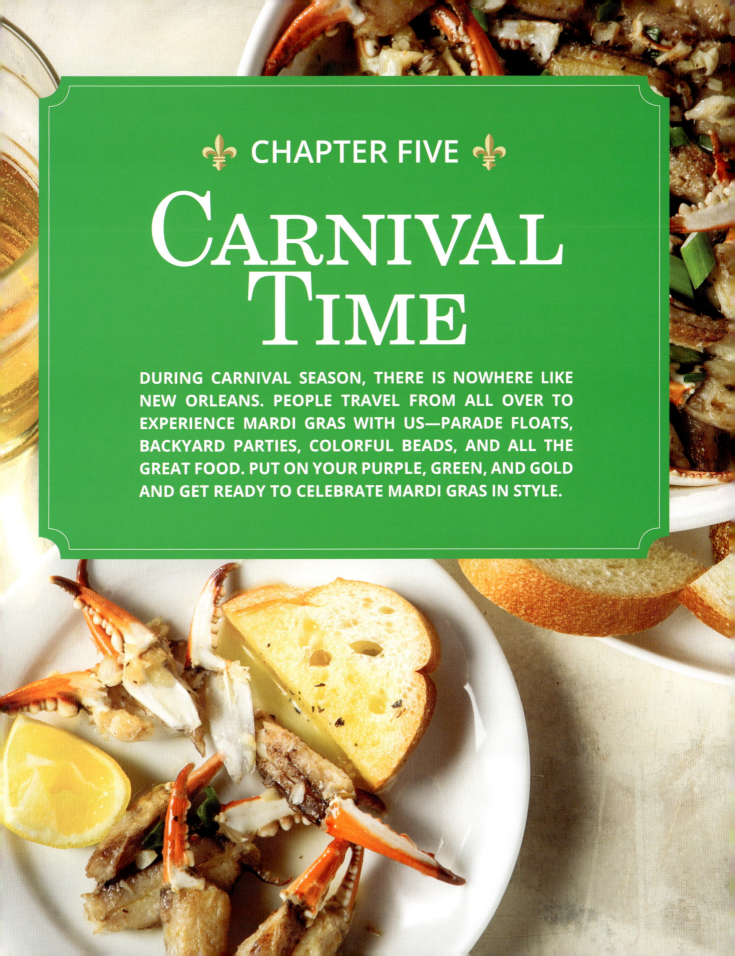

CHAPTER FIVE

CARNIVAL TIME

DURING CARNIVAL SEASON, THERE IS NOWHERE LIKE NEW ORLEANS. PEOPLE TRAVEL FROM ALL OVER TO EXPERIENCE MARDI GRAS WITH US—PARADE FLOATS, BACKYARD PARTIES, COLORFUL BEADS, AND ALL THE GREAT FOOD. PUT ON YOUR PURPLE, GREEN, AND GOLD AND GET READY TO CELEBRATE MARDI GRAS IN STYLE.

Mardi Gras Traditions

I'm the youngest of five kids and the only boy. Luckily, I'm close to my family, and we get together whenever we can, especially during holidays. If you grew up in Louisiana, you know a family gathering isn't complete without some kind of food. We can't get together without everyone bringing something. There's no such thing as too much food here!

During Mardi Gras, we try to all get together to celebrate. It's nice to go to parades and balls, but there's nothing like a backyard shrimp boil to celebrate with your family. Everyone comes over early to get the boil started, and we get to stand around outside laughing and talking while the pot boils. I put some newspaper down on folding tables and just dump the boil right on the table. No plates needed! We keep a trashcan nearby and just stand around the table and eat.

Boils are some of my favorite Mardi Gras memories. As we get older, it's a great way to celebrate Carnival as a family. ⚜

Pepper Jelly-Cheese Dip

MAKES 6 TO 9 SERVINGS

Spicy and sweet, this dip is perfect for snacking. Pair it with buttery round crackers and see how fast it gets eaten.

4 ounces sharp Cheddar cheese

4 ounces Pepper Jack cheese

2 (8-ounce) packages cream cheese, softened

1½ teaspoons dried minced onion

½ teaspoon garlic powder

½ teaspoon dried parsley

¼ teaspoon dry mustard

¼ teaspoon cayenne pepper, or to taste

¼ teaspoon celery salt

¾ cup red pepper jelly

Buttery round crackers*, to serve

1 Grate Cheddar and Pepper Jack into thick shreds, and set aside.

2 In a large bowl, beat cream cheese with a mixer at high speed until creamy, 1 to 2 minutes. Add minced onion, garlic powder, parsley, dry mustard, cayenne pepper, and celery salt, and beat until combined. Add shredded cheese a little at a time, beating until well combined. Beat for 1 minute. Cover and refrigerate overnight.

3 When ready to serve, spread cream cheese mixture onto a plate, and spread pepper jelly on top. Serve with crackers.

I use Ritz crackers.

RALPH'S TIP

I prefer to eat this dip cold, but some people love it warmed up. Spread the cream cheese mixture in a baking dish, and bake at 350° for 20 minutes until the cheese is hot and bubbly. Microwave pepper jelly until melted, and pour on top of the cheese mixture. Enjoy with crackers!

Boudin King Cake Burgers

MAKES 4

**This hamburger is salty and sweet. It's the perfect meal after a day
of catching throws at Mardi Gras parades.**

1 pound ground beef

1 large link white boudin sausage,
casing removed, crumbled

2 teaspoons RTB Hamburger Seasoning

1 teaspoon kosher salt

½ teaspoon ground black pepper

4 (1-ounce) slices Pepper Jack cheese

4 large cinnamon rolls, cut in half
horizontally (icing reserved for
assembly)

8 slices bacon, cooked

Green, yellow, and purple sanding sugar

1 Preheat an outdoor flattop griddle over medium heat.

2 In a medium bowl, combine beef, boudin, RTB Hamburger Seasoning, salt, and pepper. Shape meat mixture into 4 patties.

3 Place meat patties on griddle, and cook until a meat thermometer registers an internal temperature of 155°, 4 to 5 minutes, turning once. Place cheese on patties, and place patties on bottom half of cinnamon rolls. Top with bacon and top of cinnamon rolls. Spread icing onto each roll, and sprinkle evenly with sanding sugar.

HOT WINGS

MAKES 6 SERVINGS

The trick to good hot wings is to layer in the flavor. I start with RTB Cajun Seasoning and RTB Blackened Seasoning to get the wings nice and coated before tossing them in a spicy sauce.

3 pounds chicken wings*

2 teaspoons RTB Cajun Seasoning

2 teaspoons RTB Blackened Seasoning

1 teaspoon garlic powder

½ lemon

1½ sticks (¾ cup) unsalted butter, divided

1½ cups RTB Cajun Hot Sauce

¼ cup distilled white vinegar

2 tablespoons tomato paste

Ranch dressing, to serve

1 In a large bowl, combine chicken, RTB Cajun Seasoning, RTB Blackened Seasoning, and garlic powder. Squeeze lemon over chicken, tossing to coat.

2 Preheat an outdoor flattop griddle over medium heat. Add ½ stick (¼ cup) butter to one side of griddle. When butter melts, add chicken. Cook for 10 minutes, turning halfway through cooking. Cover and cook until golden brown and cooked through, turning once, 15 to 20 minutes.

3 While chicken cooks, place a 12-inch cast-iron skillet on other side of griddle. Add remaining 1 stick (½ cup) butter. When butter melts, add RTB Cajun Hot Sauce, vinegar, and tomato paste; stir until blended. Cook until heated through, 8 to 10 minutes.

4 In another large bowl, toss chicken with sauce until well coated. Serve with ranch dressing.

I prefer to use a mixture of flats and drumettes.

CHARGRILLED OYSTERS

MAKES 12

Filled with a garlic butter and Parmesan cheese, these oysters are full of rich flavor. Top with a little hot sauce, and you'll eat a dozen by yourself!

1 stick (½ cup) unsalted butter, softened

3 cloves garlic, minced

¼ cup chopped fresh parsley

¼ cup freshly grated Parmesan cheese

¼ cup freshly grated Romano cheese

1 tablespoon fresh lemon juice

1½ teaspoons paprika

Kosher salt and ground black pepper, to taste

12 large fresh oysters on the half shell*

Garnish: RTB Cajun Hot Sauce

1. Preheat a charcoal grill to high heat.

2. In a medium bowl, mix together butter, garlic, parsley, cheeses, lemon juice, and paprika until well combined. Add salt and pepper to taste.

3. Place oysters on a platter. Generously spoon butter mixture evenly onto each oyster until well coated, reserving extra butter mixture for dipping.

4. Carefully place each oyster, butter side up, directly on hot grill. (Be careful not to spill the butter mixture; this could ignite flames.) Grill until edges of oysters start to curl and butter mixture is bubbling and lightly browned, 5 to 7 minutes.

5. Carefully remove oysters from grill, and place on serving platter. Serve hot with reserved butter mixture. Garnish with a few dashes of RTB Cajun Hot Sauce, if desired.

*Use Gulf of Mexico oysters, if possible.

I'm close with all five of my kids, and I try to find shared interests with each of them. My oldest son has always cooked with me, and now that my youngest boys are getting older, they're starting to help more. I'm excited to teach them all that my mom taught me.

SAUTÉED CRAB CLAWS

MAKES 8 SERVINGS

Cooked in a Cajun seasoned butter sauce, these crab claws are a quick and easy appetizer for any party. I love to eat mine with French bread.

2 sticks (1 cup) unsalted butter, divided

¼ cup Italian dressing

3 tablespoons diced green onion

3 tablespoons bottled minced garlic

1 tablespoon RTB Dubba-U Sauce

1 lemon, halved

1 teaspoon dried basil

1 teaspoon RTB Cajun Seasoning

2 pounds crab claws

French bread and lemon wedges, to serve

1 In a large skillet, melt 1 stick (½ cup) butter over medium heat. Add Italian dressing, green onion, garlic, RTB Dubba-U Sauce, juice of one lemon half, basil, and RTB Cajun Seasoning, stirring to combine. Add crab claws. Add remaining 1 stick (½ cup) butter in 1-tablespoon chunks. Add remaining half of lemon, sliced into wedges. Cook for 2 minutes, gently stirring. Serve with bread and lemon wedges.

BOUDIN KING CAKE

MAKES 1 CAKE

This is a savory twist on the Mardi Gras staple. This king cake is absolutely delicious. Everyone is going to love it.

8 slices bacon

1 pound white boudin, casings removed, crumbled

1 pound cooked crawfish tail meat

1 cup chopped green onion

2 teaspoons RTB Cajun Seasoning

4 teaspoons RTB Cajun Hot Sauce, divided

2 (8-ounce) cans refrigerated crescent roll dough

5 slices Pepper Jack cheese, halved

¼ cup pepper jelly

Garnish: chopped green onion

1 Preheat oven to 350°. Line a rimmed baking sheet with parchment paper.

2 In a large Magnalite pot, cook bacon over medium heat until crispy, about 10 minutes, turning halfway through. Remove bacon, reserving drippings in pot. Crumble bacon, and set aside.

3 Add boudin, crawfish, green onion, RTB Cajun Seasoning, and 2 teaspoons RTB Cajun Hot Sauce to bacon drippings. Cook for 5 minutes, stirring occasionally. Remove from heat, and let cool slightly.

4 On prepared baking sheet, place crescent roll dough in a circle, overlapping as needed, with the base of the triangle along the outside and the tip at the center of the circle. Gently press dough together. Using a cup or a Mason jar lid, cut a small circle from the center of the circle. Discard. Spoon a ring of boudin mixture onto dough, making sure it is in the center. Add cheese, half of crumbled bacon, and remaining 2 teaspoons RTB Cajun Hot Sauce. Grab outside edge of dough ring and fold over filling, connecting to inside circle of dough and pinching to close. Repeat until all filling is covered.

5 Bake until golden brown, 25 to 30 minutes. Top with pepper jelly and remaining bacon, and garnish with green onion, if desired.

Shrimp Boil

MAKES 12 TO 15 SERVINGS

Shrimp, sausage, corn, and potatoes are the key ingredients in a good shrimp boil. Don't forget to season it up right with boil seasoning, celery, onion, garlic, and lemons!

1 (2-pound) package RTB Seafood Boil Seasoning

4 pounds small red potatoes

3 bunches celery, trimmed and stalks cut in thirds

4 unpeeled medium yellow onions, halved

10 heads garlic

4 lemons, halved

4 pounds head-on large fresh shrimp

4 pounds smoked sausage, cut into 2-inch pieces

12 mini corn cobs, frozen

Lemon wedges and melted butter, to serve

1 Place a 120-quart pot with a basket on a heavy-duty outdoor burner. Fill halfway with water. Add RTB Seafood Boil Seasoning, potatoes, celery, onion, and garlic. Squeeze lemon halves over mixture before adding into pot. Bring mixture to a rolling boil; cook until potatoes are fork-tender, about 40 minutes, stirring occasionally.

2 Add shrimp, sausage, and corn. Cook for 5 minutes. Turn off heat.

3 Using a garden hose, spray water around outside of pot, cooling mixture. Continue to stir while mixture cools.

4 Let stand for 10 to 15 minutes, allowing shrimp to absorb seasoning. Drain, and serve hot with lemon wedges and melted butter.

CAJUN CRACKLINGS

MAKES 8 SERVINGS

I like to make a big box of cracklings during Mardi Gras season. Crunchy and salty, they're the perfect snack to enjoy between parades.

3 pounds pork belly with fat attached, cut into 1-inch pieces

3 to 5 tablespoons kosher salt

Vegetable or peanut oil, for frying

2 tablespoons RTB Cajun Seasoning

2 tablespoons RTB Lemon Pepper "Alright Y'all" Seasoning

1 tablespoon chili powder

1 Pat pork dry with a paper towel. Season evenly with salt.

2 In a deep frying pan or a deep fryer, pour oil to a depth of 1½ inches, and heat over medium-high heat until a deep-fry thermometer registers 350°.

3 Fry pork in batches pork until golden brown and puffed, 2 to 3 minutes, stirring frequently. Using a slotted spoon, remove from oil, and let drain on paper towels.

4 Reheat oil to 350°, and add pork in two batches. Fry for 2 minutes, and quickly remove before burning. The pork will begin to make a light cracking sound. (This is how you know you have "cracklings.") Let drain on paper towels.

5 In a large bowl, add hot pork, RTB Cajun Seasoning, RTB Lemon Pepper "Alright Y'all" Seasoning, and chili powder; toss to coat. Let cool slightly before serving.

NOTE: *I make mine a few days ahead and store them in an airtight container. They'll be good for 5 days.*

FRIED SHRIMP PO' BOYS

MAKES 4

You can't beat a good French bread smothered in mayonnaise, loaded with fried shrimp, and topped with lettuce, tomato, and pickles. You've got to check it out, y'all!

Vegetable oil, for frying

2 pounds peeled and deveined medium fresh shrimp

3 teaspoons RTB Cajun Seasoning, divided

3 large eggs

¼ cup whole milk

2 (10-ounce) packages shrimp fry*

1 (1-pound) loaf French bread, cut into 4 portions and halved horizontally

Mayonnaise, sliced iceberg lettuce, tomato slices, and dill pickle chips, to serve

1 In a large cast-iron pot or Dutch oven, pour oil to fill halfway, and heat over medium-high heat until a deep-fry thermometer registers 350°.

2 In shallow dish, toss together shrimp and 1 teaspoon RTB Cajun Seasoning.

3 In another shallow dish, whisk together eggs, milk, and 1 teaspoon RTB Cajun Seasoning. In another shallow dish, stir together shrimp fry and remaining 1 teaspoon RTB Cajun Seasoning. Working in batches, dip shrimp in egg wash and then in shrimp fry mix, pressing to adhere.

4 Fry shrimp in batches until golden brown, 2 to 3 minutes, turning occasionally. Remove from oil, and let drain on paper towels. Serve hot on French bread with mayonnaise, lettuce, tomatoes, and pickles.

*I use Zatarain's or Louisiana Brand Seasoned Shrimp Fry.

RALPH'S TIP

For the best shrimp po' boy, fry your shrimp fresh. You don't want soggy shrimp on your sandwich. You can even put the sandwich together before you start frying to make sure it's ready to go.

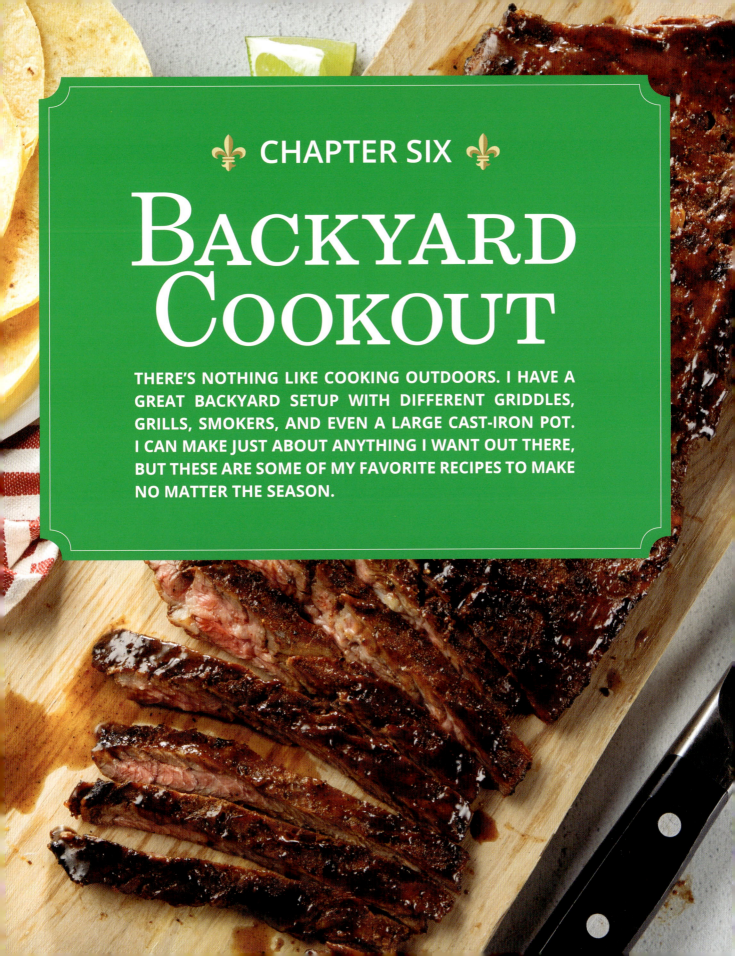

CHAPTER SIX

BACKYARD COOKOUT

THERE'S NOTHING LIKE COOKING OUTDOORS. I HAVE A GREAT BACKYARD SETUP WITH DIFFERENT GRIDDLES, GRILLS, SMOKERS, AND EVEN A LARGE CAST-IRON POT. I CAN MAKE JUST ABOUT ANYTHING I WANT OUT THERE, BUT THESE ARE SOME OF MY FAVORITE RECIPES TO MAKE NO MATTER THE SEASON.

STEAK AND CRAWFISH SANDWICHES

MAKES 6 SERVINGS

**How do you make the classic steak, pepper, and cheese sandwich even better?
Add some crawfish and RTB Cajun Seasoning!**

2 sticks (1 cup) unsalted butter, divided

1 medium yellow onion, sliced

1 medium red bell pepper, cut into ½-inch strips

1 medium green bell pepper, cut into ½-inch strips

2 teaspoons RTB Cajun Seasoning, divided

1 teaspoon kosher salt, divided

1 teaspoon ground black pepper, divided

1 (1½-pound) steak, thinly sliced

1 pound cooked crawfish tail meat

6 hoagie rolls

6 slices provolone cheese, halved

1 Preheat an outdoor flattop griddle over medium heat. Add 1 stick (½ cup) butter to one side of griddle. When butter melts, add onion, bell peppers, 1 teaspoon RTB Cajun Seasoning, ½ teaspoon salt, and ½ teaspoon pepper. Cook until tender, 7 to 8 minutes, stirring occasionally.

2 Add remaining 1 stick (½ cup) butter to other side of griddle. When butter melts, add steak and crawfish next to each other. Season with remaining 1 teaspoon RTB Cajun Seasoning, remaining ½ teaspoon salt, and remaining ½ teaspoon pepper. Cook until steak is browned or to desired degree of doneness and crawfish is heated through, stirring frequently.

3 Open rolls flat, and place, cut side down, on griddle. Cook until lightly browned, 2 to 3 minutes. Divide vegetables among bottom half of rolls. Top with steak, cheese, and crawfish. Serve hot.

RALPH'S TIP

If you're having trouble cutting your steak in thin slices, throw it in the freezer. It's a lot easier to get nice, even slices when it's a little frozen.

Fajita Bowls

MAKES 6 SERVINGS

Rice seasoned with enchilada sauce is topped with sautéed veggies and seared strips of steak. It's the perfect weeknight meal when you want something good and easy.

1 stick (½ cup) unsalted butter

1 medium green bell pepper, cut into ½-inch strips

1 medium yellow onion, cut into ¼-inch slices

1 medium red bell pepper, cut into ½-inch strips

1 lime, halved

2 teaspoons RTB Cajun Seasoning

2 beef tenderloin steaks, cut into thin slices

2 tablespoons fajita seasoning

6 cups cooked long-grain white rice, cold

1½ cups enchilada sauce

½ cup chopped fresh cilantro

Lime wedges, to serve

1 Preheat an outdoor flattop griddle over medium heat. Add butter. When butter melts, add onion and bell peppers. Squeeze 1 lime half over vegetables, and season with RTB Cajun Seasoning. Cook until tender, about 5 minutes, stirring frequently. Push onion mixture to center of griddle. Continue to stir occasionally.

2 Add beef to center of griddle, and season with fajita seasoning. Squeeze remaining lime half over beef. Cook until medium-rare, 6 to 8 minutes, stirring frequently.

3 Place rice on other side of griddle. Pour enchilada sauce over rice, and sprinkle with cilantro. Stir until combined and heated through.

4 Spoon rice into individual serving bowls. Top servings with bell pepper mixture and beef. Serve hot with lime wedges.

Shrimp and Sausage Boats

MAKES 4 SERVINGS

**With peppers, onion, shrimp, and sausage wrapped in aluminum foil,
this dinner is quick and easy with a fast cleanup.**

1½ pounds peeled and deveined
   medium fresh shrimp

2 smoked andouille sausages,
   thinly sliced

1 pound red potatoes, cut into
   1-inch pieces

2 ears corn, shucked and cut
   crosswise into 4 pieces

2 cloves garlic, minced

2 tablespoons extra-virgin olive oil

1 tablespoon RTB Cajun Seasoning

Kosher salt and ground black
   pepper, to taste

½ stick (¼ cup) unsalted butter

2 tablespoons chopped fresh parsley

1 lemon, sliced into thin wedges

Garnish: chopped fresh parsley

1 Preheat grill to high heat or preheat oven to 425°. Cut 4 sheets of heavy-duty foil about 12 inches long.

2 Divide shrimp, sausage, potatoes, corn, and garlic evenly among prepared foil sheets. Drizzle each with oil. Season each with RTB Cajun Seasoning and salt and pepper to taste, tossing gently to combine. Top each with butter, parsley, and lemon. Fold foil packets crosswise over shrimp mixture to completely cover. Roll top and side edges to seal them closed.

3 Place foil packets on grill until shrimp are just cooked through, 15 to 20 minutes; alternatively, bake for 20 minutes. Serve hot with parsley, if desired.

STEAK SLIDERS

MAKES 12 SERVINGS

These mini sandwiches are addicting! Packed with juicy steak, they're brushed with garlic and herb butter for even more flavor.

2 sticks (1 cup) garlic and herb butter, room temperature and divided

2 medium green bell peppers, thinly sliced

1 large yellow onion, thinly sliced

1 teaspoon garlic powder

1 teaspoon kosher salt, divided

1 teaspoon ground black pepper, divided

2 boneless rib eye steaks, sliced ¼ inch thick

1 (24-count) package dinner rolls

3 cups shredded Pepper Jack cheese

1 Preheat an outdoor flattop griddle over medium heat. Add 1 stick (½ cup) butter to one side of griddle. When butter melts, add bell peppers, onion, garlic powder, ½ teaspoon salt, and ½ teaspoon pepper. Cook until tender, 5 to 6 minutes, turning frequently with a metal spatula.

2 Add ½ stick (¼ cup) butter to other side of griddle. When butter melts, add steak; season with remaining ½ teaspoon salt and remaining ½ teaspoon pepper. Cook until lightly browned, 3 to 4 minutes, turning frequently.

3 Place rolls on a baking sheet. Using a serrated knife, cut rolls in half horizontally. (Do not separate individual rolls.) Spread steak over bottom half of rolls. Top with bell pepper mixture and cheese. Cover with top half of rolls. Spread remaining ½ stick (¼ cup) butter over top of rolls. Place on griddle. Cover and cook until cheese melts, 2 to 3 minutes. Serve hot.

CHICKEN AND SHRIMP FRIED RICE

MAKES 8 SERVINGS

You'll never order takeout again with this homemade version of fried rice. It's packed full of chicken, shrimp, and vegetables. It's a good one, y'all.

1 stick (½ cup) unsalted butter

2 pounds boneless skinless chicken breasts, cut into 1½-inch cubes

2 tablespoons RTB Cajun Seasoning, divided

2 tablespoons RTB Lemon Pepper "Alright Y'all" Seasoning, divided

2 teaspoons kosher salt

1 teaspoon ground black pepper

2 pounds peeled and deveined medium fresh shrimp

2 teaspoons garlic powder

2 cups cooked long-grain white rice, cold

1 medium yellow onion, chopped

1 (10-ounce) package frozen peas and carrots

¼ cup soy sauce

2 tablespoons dark sesame oil

5 large eggs, lightly beaten

1 Preheat an outdoor flattop griddle over medium heat. Add butter. When butter melts, add chicken, 1 tablespoon RTB Cajun Seasoning, 1 tablespoon RTB Lemon Pepper "Alright Y'all" Seasoning, salt, and pepper. Cook until lightly browned and a meat thermometer registers an internal temperature of 165°, stirring frequently. Push chicken to one side of griddle.

2 While chicken cooks, add shrimp, garlic powder, remaining 1 tablespoon RTB Cajun Seasoning, and remaining 1 tablespoon RTB Lemon Pepper "Alright Y'all" Seasoning to center of griddle. Cook until shrimp begin to curl and turn pink, 1 to 2 minutes per side. Push shrimp to side with chicken.

3 While shrimp cooks, add rice, onion, peas and carrots, soy sauce, and sesame oil to griddle. Add eggs, and cook until set, stirring frequently. Using a large metal spatula, stir together chicken, shrimp, rice, and eggs until well combined. Serve hot.

HONEY BUFFALO FRIED CHICKEN STRIPS

MAKES 8 TO 10 SERVINGS

These chicken strips are the perfect blend of juicy, crispy, sweet, and spicy. Fried to perfection, they're then coated in a honey Buffalo sauce. The kids love this one!

Vegetable oil, for frying

3 cups all-purpose flour

3 tablespoons RTB Cajun Seasoning, divided

2 tablespoons onion powder, divided

2 tablespoons smoked paprika, divided

2 teaspoons kosher salt, divided

1 teaspoon ground black pepper, divided

1 cup whole milk

2 large eggs

3 pounds chicken tenderloins

½ cup Buffalo wing sauce

¼ cup honey

Garnish: chopped fresh parsley

1 Preheat an outdoor flattop griddle over medium heat. Place a large cast-iron pan on griddle. Pour oil to a depth of 1 inch, and heat until a deep-fry thermometer registers 350°. Line a baking sheet with paper towels; top with a wire rack.

2 In a shallow pan, whisk together flour, 2 tablespoons RTB Cajun Seasoning, 1 tablespoon onion powder, 1 tablespoon smoked paprika, 1 teaspoon salt, and ½ teaspoon pepper.

3 In a medium bowl, whisk together milk and eggs.

4 Evenly season chicken with remaining 1 tablespoon RTB Cajun Seasoning, remaining 1 tablespoon onion powder, remaining 1 tablespoon smoked paprika, remaining 1 teaspoon salt, and remaining ½ teaspoon pepper.

5 Working in batches, dredge chicken in flour mixture and then dip in egg mixture, letting excess drip off. Dredge in flour mixture again, pressing to adhere.

6 Fry chicken in batches until golden brown and a meat thermometer registers an internal temperature of 165°, 3 to 4 minutes, turning occasionally. Remove from oil, and let drain on a wire rack.

7 In a bowl, stir together wing sauce and honey. Drizzle over chicken. Serve hot with parsley, if desired.

Carne Asada

MAKES 6 TO 8 SERVINGS

Marinated in beer, lime juice, jalapeños, and seasoning, carne asada is overflowing with flavor. Slice it up and serve it on tortillas for the perfect tacos.

1½ pounds skirt steak

6 (12-ounce) cans pilsner-style Mexican lager beer*

7 limes, juiced

2 large jalapeños, sliced

¼ cup chopped fresh cilantro

1½ tablespoons chili powder

1 tablespoon RTB Cajun Seasoning

1 tablespoon garlic powder

1 tablespoon paprika

1 teaspoon kosher salt

1 teaspoon ground black pepper

1 stick (½ cup) unsalted butter

Corn tortillas, chopped onion, jalapeños, and lime wedges, to serve

1 In a large container, add steak, beer, lime juice, jalapeños, cilantro, chili powder, RTB Cajun Seasoning, garlic powder, paprika, salt, and pepper. Cover and marinate in refrigerator for 2 hours.

2 Preheat an outdoor flattop griddle over medium heat. Add butter. When butter melts, add marinated meat to griddle. Cook until steak is cooked to medium to medium-rare, 6 to 8 minutes, turning occasionally. Remove from griddle, and slice into 3- to 4-inch strips. Serve with tortillas, chopped onion, jalapeños, and lime wedges.

I use Modelo.

Taco Burgers

MAKES 8

There is a place near me that used to make these massive taco burgers, but now, they're more like sliders. I loved the old ones so much, I learned to make them myself.

1 stick (½ cup) unsalted butter

3 pounds ground beef

2 (1-ounce) packages taco seasoning

2 teaspoons RTB Cajun Seasoning

½ teaspoon ground black pepper

1 medium yellow onion

Hamburger buns, sliced iceberg lettuce, shredded Cheddar cheese, chopped tomato, and RTB Cajun Hot Sauce, to serve

1 Preheat an outdoor flattop griddle over medium heat. Add butter. When butter melts, add beef, taco seasoning, RTB Cajun Seasoning, and pepper to one side of griddle. Cook until browned and crumbly, 8 to 9 minutes, stirring occasionally.

2 While beef cooks, add onion to other side of griddle. Cook until lightly browned, about 5 minutes, stirring occasionally. Stir together beef and onion. Serve on buns with lettuce, cheese, tomato, and RTB Cajun Hot Sauce.

MEXICAN STREET CORN NACHOS

MAKES 6 TO 8 SERVINGS

I love to make this platter of nachos for a crowd to enjoy. Make sure to be generous with the chile lime seasoning!

1 stick (½ cup) unsalted butter

2 pounds ground beef

½ teaspoon onion powder

½ teaspoon RTB Cajun Seasoning

Kosher salt and ground black pepper, to taste

1 medium yellow onion, diced

1 large jalapeño, seeded and diced

2 cups frozen corn kernels, thawed

1 teaspoon chile lime seasoning*

½ cup mayonnaise

2 tablespoons fresh lime juice

1 (16-ounce) bag tortilla chips

3 tablespoons Mexican sour cream*

1 cup crumbled queso fresco

¼ cup chopped fresh cilantro

½ lime

1. Preheat an outdoor flattop griddle over medium heat. Add butter. When butter melts, add beef, onion powder, RTB Cajun Seasoning, and salt and black pepper to taste. Cook until beef is browned and crumbly, 8 to 9 minutes, stirring occasionally. Push to one side of griddle.

2. Add onion, jalapeño, corn, and chile lime seasoning to other side of griddle. Cook until vegetables are tender, about 5 minutes, stirring occasionally.

3. In a bowl, combine mayonnaise and lime juice. Set aside.

4. On a large platter, layer tortilla chips, beef mixture, and vegetable mixture. Drizzle with mayonnaise mixture and sour cream. Sprinkle queso fresco and cilantro on top. Squeeze lime juice over nachos.

I use Tajín Clássico and Cacique Crema Mexicana.

SMASHBURGERS

MAKES 2

If you've never had a smashburger before, you've got to try these. The edges get a crispy brown crust that make each bite better than the last.

14 ounces ground beef

Kosher salt, ground black pepper, and RTB Dubba-U Sauce, to taste

¼ cup vegetable oil

½ medium white onion, chopped

2 slices Cheddar cheese

Ketchup, yellow mustard, and mayonnaise, to taste

2 sesame seed buns

6 leaves iceberg lettuce

10 dill pickle slices

4 slices tomato

1 Season beef with salt and pepper to taste. Add a few dashes of RTB Dubba-U Sauce, and form into 4 equal balls. Flatten meatballs by stacking them between pieces of parchment paper and then pressing them down with a flat hamburger press or spatula. Place 1 patty on top of a piece of parchment paper and then top with another piece of paper, another patty, and another piece of paper. Squash it all down with a hamburger press or spatula. Repeat with remaining patties.

2 Preheat an outdoor flattop griddle over medium heat. Add oil. Place patties and onion on griddle. Cook patties for about 2 minutes per side, stirring onion in the meantime so it cooks evenly. Place 1 slice Cheddar each on 2 patties.

3 Meanwhile, make three rings of ketchup and two rings of mustard on bottom half of each bun, and spread mayonnaise on top half of each bun.

4 Place equal amounts of fried onions on top of ketchup and mustard on bottom half of each bun. Add cheese-covered patty to each bun, and top each with a second patty. Place equal amounts of lettuce, pickle slices, and tomato slices, if desired on top of patties. Place top half of each bun on top. Serve hot.

RALPH'S TIP —————————

A lot of people like to swap out lower-fat ground beef to try and be healthier. This is not the recipe to do it with. If you use anything less than 80% fat, you'll end up with dry burgers.

TOMAHAWK STEAK WITH SHRIMP

MAKES 4

Steak seared and then basted in butter, garlic, and rosemary paired with blackened shrimp is the perfect dinner for any special occasion.

2½ sticks (1¼ cups) unsalted butter, divided

1 (2-pound) tomahawk steak

1 tablespoon RTB Steak Seasoning

2 teaspoons kosher salt

1 teaspoon ground black pepper

2 tablespoons fresh rosemary leaves

4 teaspoons minced garlic

1 pound peeled and deveined medium fresh shrimp

1 tablespoon RTB Blackened Seasoning

1 Preheat an outdoor flattop griddle over medium heat. Add 1 stick (½ cup) butter.

2 While butter melts, season both sides of steak with RTB Steak Seasoning, salt, and pepper. Add seasoned steak to griddle. Cook for 6 minutes, turning halfway. Add 1 stick (½ cup) butter, rosemary, and garlic to top of steak. Cover with foil. Cook for 5 minutes. Remove foil, and sear sides of steak, about 5 minutes per side. Place on one side of griddle, continuing to cook until desired doneness is reached.

3 While steak cooks, add remaining ½ stick (¼ cup) butter to other side of griddle. When butter melts, add shrimp and season with RTB Blackened Seasoning. Cook until shrimp begin to curl and turn pink, 1 to 2 minutes per side. Serve hot.

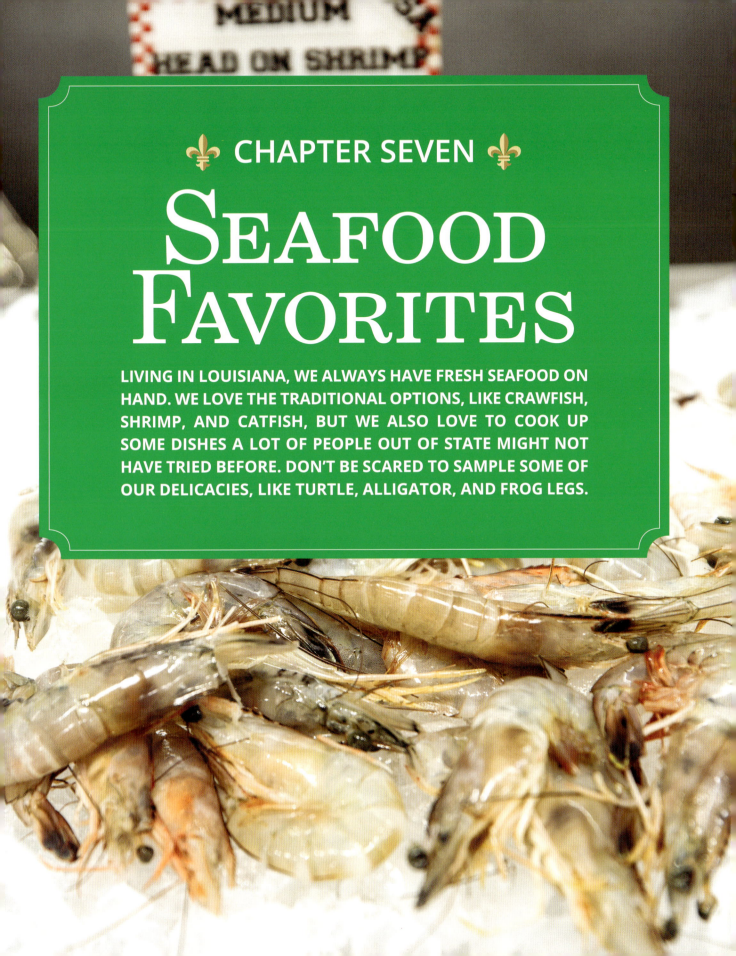

CHAPTER SEVEN

SEAFOOD FAVORITES

LIVING IN LOUISIANA, WE ALWAYS HAVE FRESH SEAFOOD ON HAND. WE LOVE THE TRADITIONAL OPTIONS, LIKE CRAWFISH, SHRIMP, AND CATFISH, BUT WE ALSO LOVE TO COOK UP SOME DISHES A LOT OF PEOPLE OUT OF STATE MIGHT NOT HAVE TRIED BEFORE. DON'T BE SCARED TO SAMPLE SOME OF OUR DELICACIES, LIKE TURTLE, ALLIGATOR, AND FROG LEGS.

SHRIMP AND GRITS

MAKES 8 SERVINGS

Cheesy grits smothered in shrimp and sauce make this the ultimate comfort meal. Plus, it comes together quickly, so you'll have dinner ready in no time! My kids love this one.

GRITS:

4 cups chicken broth

1 cup stone-ground grits

Kosher salt and ground black pepper, to taste

1 cup shredded sharp Cheddar cheese (optional)

2 tablespoons salted butter

SHRIMP:

1 pound bacon, chopped

½ stick (¼ cup) unsalted butter

2 pounds peeled and deveined large fresh shrimp

2 cloves garlic, minced

1 lemon, juiced

2 tablespoons RTB Dubba-U Sauce

4 green onions, sliced and divided

¼ cup chicken broth

2 tablespoons RTB Cajun Seasoning

1½ teaspoons smoked paprika

Kosher salt and ground black pepper, to taste

1 **For grits:** In a medium saucepan, bring chicken broth to a boil over high heat. Stir in grits, and reduce heat to low. Cook until they are creamy and tender, 20 to 25 minutes, stirring occasionally. Season to taste with salt and pepper. Stir in cheese (if using) and butter until melted and well combined. Keep warm.

2 **For shrimp:** In a large skillet, cook bacon over medium heat until crispy, 5 to 6 minutes, stirring frequently. Remove bacon, reserving drippings in skillet, and let drain on paper towels.

3 In same skillet, melt butter over medium heat. Add shrimp, garlic, lemon juice, and RTB Dubba-U Sauce. Cook until shrimp begin to curl and turn pink, 1 to 2 minutes per side. Stir in half of green onion, chicken broth, RTB Cajun Seasoning, paprika, and salt and pepper to taste. Cook for 2 to 3 minutes. Add ¾ cup cooked bacon, stirring to combine. Serve shrimp mixture and sauce hot over prepared grits. Top with remaining green onion and remaining cooked bacon.

RALPH'S TIP

Grits are best eaten fresh, but if you have extra, don't worry. The leftovers are salvageable. Put them in a saucepan over medium heat with a few tablespoons of chicken broth. Slowly warm it up, stirring as you go. They'll be creamy and ready in no time.

BLACKENED CATFISH

MAKES 6 TO 12 SERVINGS

Each fillet is coated in my RTB Blackened Seasoning, which gives it the perfect smoky and spicy flavor. Squeeze on a little lemon juice at the end to make it even better.

¾ cup RTB Cajun Seasoning

¼ cup RTB Blackened Seasoning

2 tablespoons ground white pepper

2 tablespoons paprika

2 tablespoons cayenne pepper

6 to 12 catfish fillets

2 tablespoons unsalted butter

Lemon wedges, to serve

1 In a large bowl, mix together RTB Cajun Seasoning, RTB Blackened Seasoning, white pepper, paprika, and cayenne pepper. Add fish, tossing to coat completely.

2 Preheat stovetop griddle (or an outdoor flattop griddle) over medium heat. Add butter. When butter melts, add fish, and cook until they smoke and appear blackened, 1 to 2 minutes per side.

3 Reduce heat to low. Cook, covered, for about 10 minutes. Squeeze lemon juice evenly over each fillet. Serve hot.

FRIED ALLIGATOR

MAKES 4 SERVINGS

If you've never tried alligator, this is a great recipe to start with. Whether you're using fresh or frozen alligator, these bites are crispy on the outside and moist on the inside.

1 pound boneless alligator meat, cubed

5 tablespoons RTB Cajun Seasoning, divided

2 teaspoons garlic powder

5 dashes RTB Cajun Hot Sauce

3 cups all-vegetable shortening

1 cup whole buttermilk

1 tablespoon yellow mustard, plus more to serve

1 large egg

3 cups all-purpose flour

1 Pat alligator dry with paper towels. In a medium bowl, combine alligator, 2 tablespoons RTB Cajun Seasoning, garlic powder, and RTB Cajun Hot Sauce, tossing to coat evenly. Cover and marinate for 10 minutes at room temperature.

2 Remove alligator, discarding marinade.

3 In a large cast-iron skillet, heat shortening over medium-high heat until a deep-fry thermometer registers 350°.

4 In another medium bowl, whisk together buttermilk, mustard, and egg. In a third medium bowl, whisk together flour and remaining 3 tablespoons RTB Cajun Seasoning. Dredge alligator in flour mixture, shaking off excess. Dip in buttermilk mixture, letting excess drip off. Dredge in flour mixture again.

5 Add alligator to shortening, and fry for 8 to 10 minutes, stirring occasionally. Remove from oil, and let drain on paper towels. Serve hot with mustard.

Cajun Smothered Squash with Shrimp

MAKES 6 SERVINGS

**Tender squash, spicy shrimp, and a large heaping of Cajun flavors
make this dish a summer staple in our house.**

2 tablespoons olive oil, divided

1 pound peeled and deveined
   medium fresh shrimp

2 stalks celery, chopped

1 medium yellow onion, finely chopped

1 medium red bell pepper, diced

3 cloves garlic, minced

2 tablespoons RTB Cajun Seasoning,
   or to taste

1 teaspoon dried thyme

1 teaspoon dried oregano

Kosher salt and ground black pepper,
   to taste

3 medium yellow squash, sliced

1 (14-ounce) can diced tomatoes

1 cup chicken broth

2 tablespoons tomato paste

Hot cooked white rice, to serve

1 In a large skillet, heat 1 tablespoon oil over medium-high heat. Add shrimp, and cook until shrimp begin to curl and turn pink, 1 to 2 minutes per side. Remove shrimp from skillet, and set aside.

2 In same skillet, heat remaining 1 tablespoon oil over medium-high heat. Add celery, onion, and bell pepper. Cook until tender, about 5 minutes, stirring occasionally. Stir in garlic, and cook for 1 to 2 minutes. Season with RTB Cajun Seasoning, thyme, oregano, and salt and pepper to taste. Add cooked shrimp and squash. Add diced tomatoes, chicken broth, and tomato paste, stirring to combine. Bring mixture to a simmer and then reduce heat to low. Cover and let simmer until vegetables are tender, 15 to 20 minutes. Taste and adjust seasonings if needed. Serve hot over rice.

Spicy Honey-Garlic Salmon

MAKES 2 SERVINGS

This is one of my favorite ways to cook salmon. The honey and crushed red pepper give it a great flavor. Everybody loves it.

2 sticks (1 cup) unsalted butter, divided

2 (6-ounce) salmon fillets, skinned

1 tablespoon honey hickory rub

2½ teaspoons kosher salt, divided

2½ teaspoons ground black pepper, divided

½ teaspoon crushed red pepper

3 tablespoons minced garlic, divided

2 tablespoons honey

¼ cup chopped fresh parsley

6 lemon slices

1 pound fresh asparagus, trimmed

1 teaspoon RTB Cajun Seasoning

Garnish: chopped fresh parsley

1 Preheat an outdoor flattop griddle over medium heat. Add 1 stick (½ cup) butter to one side of griddle. When butter melts, add salmon. Season with honey hickory rub, 2 teaspoons salt, 2 teaspoons black pepper, and crushed red pepper. Top with 2 tablespoons garlic, and drizzle with honey. Top with parsley and lemon slices. Cook until fish flakes with a fork, about 6 minutes.

2 While salmon is cooking, add remaining 1 stick (½ cup) butter to other side of griddle. When butter melts, add asparagus. Season with RTB Cajun Seasoning, remaining ½ teaspoon salt, and ½ teaspoon black pepper. Top with remaining 1 tablespoon garlic. Cover and cook until asparagus is tender, about 10 minutes, stirring once. Serve hot with parsley, if desired.

Tony's Seafood is a popular seafood market in Baton Rouge, Louisiana, near where one of my sisters lives. It's famous around Louisiana for having some of the freshest seafood money can buy and a good variety. I try to visit whenever I get a chance. You can get your fish from your chain grocery stores, but it's always better from a local market.

SHRIMP RÉMOULADE

MAKES 6 SERVINGS

Rémoulade is a creamy, spicy sauce that's popular in New Orleans. A lot of people like to toss their shrimp in it, but my family prefers to use it like a dipping sauce.

RÉMOULADE SAUCE:

1 cup mayonnaise

2 green onions, finely chopped

2 tablespoons chopped fresh parsley

2 tablespoons Dijon mustard

2 tablespoons whole-grain mustard

2 tablespoons ketchup

1 tablespoon RTB Cajun Hot Sauce

1½ teaspoons prepared horseradish

1 teaspoon celery seed

1 teaspoon paprika

1 teaspoon RTB Dubba-U Sauce

Kosher salt and ground black pepper, to taste

SHRIMP:

1 pound peeled and deveined (tails left on) large fresh shrimp

1 tablespoon olive oil

Kosher salt and ground black pepper, to taste

Lemon wedges, to serve

Garnish: chopped fresh parsley

1 **For rémoulade sauce:** In a medium bowl, whisk together mayonnaise, green onion, parsley, mustards, ketchup, RTB Cajun Hot Sauce, horseradish, celery seed, paprika, RTB Dubba-U Sauce, and salt and pepper to taste. Taste and adjust seasonings if needed. (If you prefer it spicier, add more hot sauce or horseradish.) Cover and refrigerate for at least 30 minutes to allow flavors to blend.

2 **For shrimp:** Preheat a large skillet over medium-high heat. Toss shrimp with olive oil, and season to taste with salt and pepper. Add shrimp to skillet, and cook until shrimp begin to curl and turn pink, 2 to 3 minutes per side. Remove shrimp from skillet, and let cool. Arrange cooked shrimp on a serving platter. Serve with chilled rémoulade sauce and lemon wedges. Garnish with parsley, if desired.

SEAFOOD POTATOES

MAKES 6 SERVINGS

I love loaded baked potatoes, especially when they are smothered in a rich and creamy cheese sauce and topped with shrimp and crawfish.

1 stick (½ cup) unsalted butter

1 pound peeled and deveined medium fresh shrimp

2 tablespoons RTB Cajun Seasoning

1 tablespoon garlic powder

2 teaspoons kosher salt

1 teaspoon ground black pepper

1 pound cooked crawfish tails

2 cups whole milk

¼ cup all-purpose flour

1 (8-ounce) container heavy whipping cream

1 cup shredded Cheddar cheese

2 teaspoons RTB Cajun Hot Sauce

Hot baked potatoes and chopped fresh parsley, to serve

1 Preheat an outdoor flattop griddle over medium heat. Add butter to one side of griddle. When butter melts, add shrimp, RTB Cajun Seasoning, garlic powder, salt, and pepper, stirring to combine. Cook until shrimp begin to curl and turn pink, 1 to 2 minutes per side.

2 While shrimp cook, add crawfish to center of griddle. Cook until warmed through, 3 to 5 minutes, stirring occasionally. Push to side with shrimp. Stir to combine.

3 While shrimp and crawfish cook, add a 12-inch cast-iron skillet to other side of griddle. Add milk and flour to skillet, stirring to combine. Add cream, cheese, and RTB Cajun Hot Sauce, stirring until cheese is melted and sauce is smooth. Serve seafood mixture and cheese sauce hot on split potatoes, and top with parsley.

Frog Legs

MAKES 6 SERVINGS

A lot of people like to fry their frog legs, but I love them grilled with hot sauce on top.

1 stick (½ cup) unsalted butter

6 pairs large frog legs

2 teaspoons RTB Dubba-U Sauce

1 teaspoon kosher salt

1 teaspoon RTB Lemon Pepper "Alright Y'all" Seasoning

1 teaspoon RTB Cajun Seasoning

1 teaspoon RTB Blackened Seasoning

½ teaspoon ground black pepper

RTB Cajun Hot Sauce, to serve

1 Preheat an outdoor flattop griddle over medium heat. Add butter. When butter melts, add frog legs. Season with RTB Dubba-U Sauce, salt, RTB Lemon Pepper "Alright Y'all" Seasoning, RTB Cajun Seasoning, RTB Blackened Seasoning, and pepper, stirring to coat both sides.

2 Cook until a meat thermometer registers an internal temperature of 145°, about 10 minutes, stirring occasionally. Serve hot with RTB Cajun Hot Sauce.

SEAFOOD CAJUN LASAGNA

MAKES 8 TO 10 SERVINGS

Lasagna in any form is good, but this one is my favorite. With sausage, shrimp, crawfish, and Pepper Jack cheese, this is some of the best lasagna ever.

1 stick (½ cup) unsalted butter

1 cup chopped yellow onion

1 cup chopped celery

1 cup chopped green bell pepper

1 pound andouille sausage, sliced

2 pounds peeled and deveined medium fresh shrimp

1 pound cooked crawfish tails

2 teaspoons RTB Cajun Seasoning, divided

2 (28-ounce) cans crushed tomatoes

1 (8-ounce) can tomato paste

1 teaspoon white sugar

1 teaspoon kosher salt

1 teaspoon garlic powder

1 teaspoon dried Italian seasoning

1 teaspoon ground black pepper

10 oven-ready lasagna noodles

1 cup shredded Pepper Jack cheese

1 cup shredded part-skim mozzarella cheese

1 cup shredded Parmesan cheese

1 cup shredded sharp Cheddar cheese

1 Preheat oven to 350°.

2 In a large Magnalite pot, melt butter over medium heat. Add onion, celery, and bell pepper. Cook until softened, 5 to 7 minutes, stirring occasionally. Add sausage, and cook until lightly browned, 8 to 10 minutes, stirring occasionally. Add shrimp, and cook until shrimp begin to curl and turn pink, 2 to 3 minutes, stirring occasionally. Stir in crawfish and 1 teaspoon RTB Cajun Seasoning.

3 In a deep skillet, combine crushed tomatoes, tomato paste, sugar, salt, garlic powder, Italian seasoning, pepper, and remaining 1 teaspoon RTB Cajun Seasoning. Cook over medium heat until heated through, about 15 minutes, stirring occasionally. Stir into shrimp mixture.

4 In a 13x9-inch baking dish, spoon 1 cup shrimp mixture. Top with 5 noodles. Spoon half of remaining shrimp mixture over noodles, spreading evenly. Sprinkle with half of cheeses. Repeat layers once. Cover with foil. Place pan on a rimmed baking sheet.

5 Bake for 35 minutes. Uncover and bake until bubbly and lightly browned, about 15 minutes more. Let cool for 10 minutes before serving.

SWEET AND SOUR TURTLE

MAKES ABOUT 8 SERVINGS

**Turtle meat isn't always easy to find, but it's worth the search for this dish.
This is the only way you'll ever want to eat turtle!**

2 sticks (1 cup) unsalted butter, divided

**2 pounds boneless turtle meat,
cut into 1½-inch cubes**

2 tablespoons RTB Cajun Seasoning

**2½ teaspoons garlic powder,
divided**

**¾ teaspoon ground black pepper,
divided**

2 medium green bell peppers, chopped

1 medium red bell pepper, chopped

2 stalks celery, chopped

1 large yellow onion, diced

**1 (20-ounce) can diced pineapples,
juice drained and reserved**

1 (8-ounce) can tomato sauce

1 cup firmly packed light brown sugar

½ teaspoon kosher salt

Hot cooked rice, to serve

1 Preheat an outdoor flattop griddle over medium heat. Add 1 stick (½ cup) butter to one side of griddle. When butter melts, add turtle, RTB Cajun Seasoning, 2 teaspoons garlic powder, and ½ teaspoon pepper. Cook until turtle is browned throughout, about 15 minutes, stirring occasionally.

2 While turtle cooks, add remaining 1 stick (½ cup) butter to center of griddle. When butter melts, add bell peppers, celery, and onion. Cook until tender, about 10 minutes, stirring occasionally. Add diced pineapple.

3 On other side of griddle, place a 13x9-inch metal pan. Add reserved pineapple juice, tomato sauce, brown sugar, salt, remaining ½ teaspoon garlic powder, and remaining ¼ teaspoon pepper, stirring until combined and sugar is dissolved. Add turtle and vegetables, and stir. Serve hot over rice.

RALPH'S TIP

Like alligator meat, turtle meat is a delicacy here in Louisiana, but it can sometimes be hard to find. If you can't get it near you, substitute it 1:1 for boneless skinless chicken thighs. Chicken doesn't have the same savoriness as turtle, but it'll still be delicious!

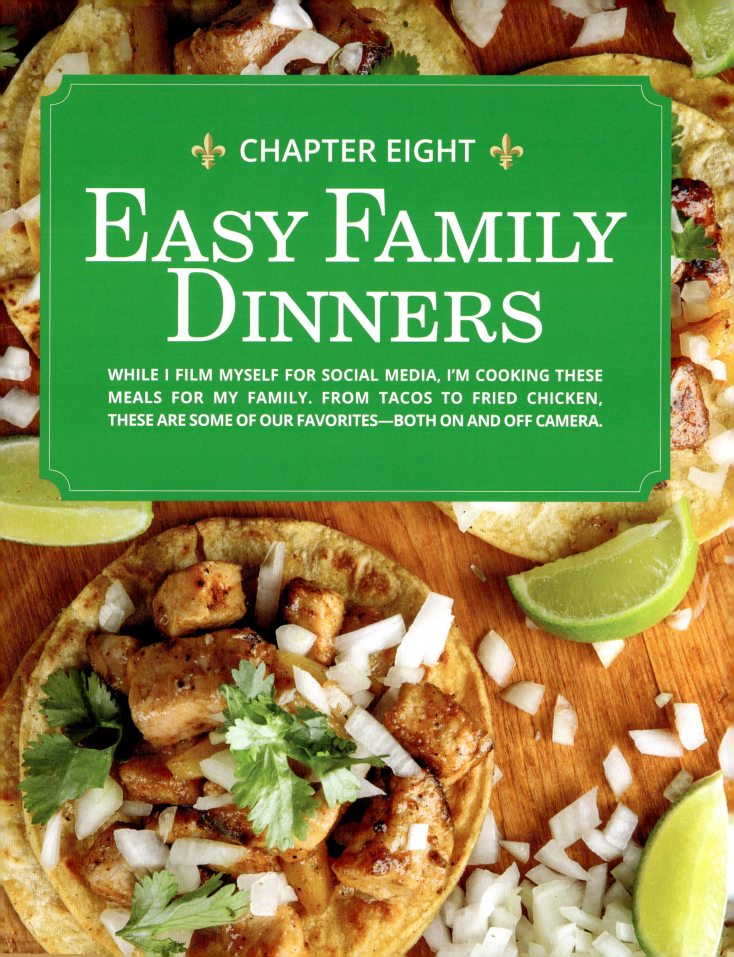

CHAPTER EIGHT

EASY FAMILY DINNERS

WHILE I FILM MYSELF FOR SOCIAL MEDIA, I'M COOKING THESE MEALS FOR MY FAMILY. FROM TACOS TO FRIED CHICKEN, THESE ARE SOME OF OUR FAVORITES—BOTH ON AND OFF CAMERA.

CABBAGE ROLLS

MAKES 21

Tender cabbage is wrapped around a hearty meat and rice filling and then smothered in a flavorful tomato sauce. It's an easy dinner that is perfect for any night of the week.

1 large head cabbage

1 pound lean ground beef

1 pound lean ground pork

2 cups chopped yellow onion

2 cups chopped green bell pepper

1 cup cooked long-grain white rice

1 (6-ounce) can tomato paste

3 cloves garlic, minced

1 teaspoon kosher salt, divided

½ teaspoon cayenne pepper, divided

¼ teaspoon ground allspice, divided

4 (12-ounce) cans tomato sauce

1 teaspoon white sugar

1 cup water

1 In a large pot, bring cabbage and water to cover to a boil over medium-high heat; cover and cook until cabbage is slightly tender, about 10 minutes. Drain well, and let cool completely. Set aside.

2 Preheat oven to 375°.

3 In a large bowl, mix beef, pork, onion, bell pepper, rice, tomato paste, garlic, ½ teaspoon salt, ¼ teaspoon cayenne pepper, and ⅛ teaspoon allspice until well combined. Set aside.

4 Gently separate cooked cabbage leaves, being careful not to tear them. Spoon 2 to 3 tablespoons meat mixture into each cabbage leaf. Gently roll up, and tuck ends of cabbage leaves under to prevent filling from falling out.

5 In a large roasting pan, place stuffed cabbage rolls, and cover with tomato sauce. Season with sugar, remaining ½ teaspoon salt, remaining ¼ teaspoon cayenne pepper, and remaining ⅛ teaspoon allspice. Add 1 cup water, and cover with foil.

6 Bake until rice becomes tender and meat is cooked, about 1 hour and 15 minutes, basting occasionally with pan juices. Serve hot.

FRIED CHICKEN

MAKES 6 SERVINGS

My secret to juicy fried chicken is an overnight buttermilk brine. This is the best chicken you'll ever make. I like to eat mine with Baked Macaroni & Cheese (see page 222).

2 cups whole buttermilk

2 tablespoons kosher salt, divided, plus more to taste

2 tablespoons RTB Cajun Seasoning, divided

2 tablespoons RTB Cajun Hot Sauce (optional)

1½ tablespoons garlic powder, divided

1½ tablespoons onion powder, divided

1½ tablespoons smoked paprika, divided

1½ tablespoons ground black pepper, divided

1½ teaspoons dried dill

1½ teaspoons cayenne pepper, divided

4 pounds chicken pieces (drumsticks, thighs, breasts, or a mix)

2 cups all-purpose flour

Vegetable or peanut oil, for frying

1 In a large bowl, whisk together buttermilk, 1 tablespoon salt, 1 tablespoon RTB Cajun Seasoning, RTB Cajun Hot Sauce (if using), ½ tablespoon garlic powder, ½ tablespoon onion powder, ½ tablespoon paprika, ½ tablespoon black pepper, dill, and ½ teaspoon cayenne pepper. Add chicken, tossing to coat. Cover and refrigerate for at least 4 hours or overnight for the best flavor.

2 In another large bowl, whisk together flour, remaining 1 tablespoon salt, remaining 1 tablespoon RTB Cajun Seasoning, remaining 1 tablespoon garlic powder, remaining 1 tablespoon onion powder, remaining 1 tablespoon paprika, remaining 1 tablespoon black pepper, and remaining 1 teaspoon cayenne pepper.

3 Remove chicken from buttermilk mixture, letting any excess drip off. Dredge each piece of chicken in flour mixture, pressing to coat. Place coated chicken on a baking sheet or wire rack, and let sit, 20 to 30 minutes. (This allows the coating to better stick to the chicken.)

4 In a large heavy-bottomed skillet or Dutch oven, pour oil to a depth of 2 inches, and heat over medium-high heat until a deep-fry thermometer registers 350°.

5 Fry chicken in batches until evenly golden brown and a meat thermometer registers an internal temperature of 165°, 12 to 15 minutes, turning chicken occasionally. (Do not overcrowd pan.) (See note.) Using a slotted spoon, remove chicken from oil, and let drain on paper towels. Sprinkle with salt to taste. Serve hot.

NOTE: *To ensure even cooking, use a deep-fry thermometer to check that the oil is still between 350°. If it isn't, allow to come back up to temperature.*

Soy Sauce and Garlic Salmon and Vegetables

MAKES 6 SERVINGS

Soy sauce, lemon, and a rich butter sauce make this light, flaky salmon hard to resist.

1 stick (½ cup) unsalted butter

3 cups sliced zucchini

3 cups sliced yellow squash

1 cup sliced red onion

4 tablespoons soy sauce, divided

6 teaspoons RTB Cajun Seasoning, divided

1 teaspoon kosher salt, divided

1 teaspoon ground black pepper, divided

1 (1½-pound) salmon fillet, skinned

1 stick (½ cup) salted butter, melted

2 tablespoons minced garlic

2 tablespoons chopped parsley

6 lemon slices

1 Preheat an outdoor flattop griddle over medium heat. Add unsalted butter. When butter melts, add zucchini, squash, onion, 2 tablespoons soy sauce, 1 teaspoon RTB Cajun Seasoning, ½ teaspoon salt, and ½ teaspoon pepper to one side of griddle. Cook until tender, about 8 minutes, stirring occasionally.

2 Place salmon on other side of griddle.

3 In a small bowl, combine melted salted butter, garlic, parsley, and 3 teaspoons RTB Cajun Seasoning. Pour over salmon. Season with remaining 2 tablespoons soy sauce, remaining 2 teaspoons RTB Cajun Seasoning, remaining ½ teaspoon salt, and remaining ½ teaspoon pepper. Top salmon with lemon slices. Cook until fish flakes easily with a fork, 8 to 10 minutes per side for medium doneness. Serve hot with zucchini mixture.

RALPH'S TIP

The key to cooking salmon on a griddle is making sure your surface is well oiled before you place the salmon; otherwise, it will stick. The butter left over from cooking the veggies should be enough to keep your salmon from sticking, but you can always add extra oil to be safe.

Cajun Stuffed Bell Peppers

MAKES 8 SERVINGS

Easy and filling, this classic dish takes green bell peppers and fills them with seasoned rice and beef.

2 tablespoons vegetable oil

1½ pounds ground beef

Kosher salt, garlic powder,
    onion powder, RTB Cajun
    Seasoning, and ground
    black pepper, to taste

2 stalks celery, finely chopped

1 medium yellow onion, chopped

1 medium green or red bell pepper,
    finely chopped

2 to 3 cups hot cooked white rice

½ stick (¼ cup) unsalted butter

8 medium green bell peppers,
    stemmed and cored

Italian-seasoned bread crumbs,
    to taste

1 In medium skillet, heat oil over medium-high heat. Add beef, and season to taste with salt, garlic powder, onion powder, RTB Cajun Seasoning, and pepper. Cook until beef is browned and crumbly, 8 to 9 minutes, stirring occasionally. Remove from skillet, and drain.

2 In same skillet, add celery, onion, and chopped bell pepper. Cook until vegetables are tender, 5 to 6 minutes, stirring occasionally. Add beef, and cook for 5 minutes, stirring frequently. Stir in rice until desired consistency is reached. (The dish will look very similar to dirty rice.) Stir in butter until melted and combined. Taste and adjust seasonings if needed.

3 Preheat oven to 300°. Add ⅛ inch water to a 13x9-inch baking dish.

4 In a large saucepan, place green bell peppers and water to cover. Bring to a boil, and cook until peppers are slightly softened, 3 to 5 minutes.

5 Remove bell peppers from water, and fill with beef mixture. Place in prepared baking dish, and cover with foil.

6 Bake for 15 minutes. Uncover and sprinkle bread crumbs evenly on top of bell peppers. Bake for 10 to 15 minutes more. Serve hot.

Coconut Shrimp

MAKES 6 SERVINGS

The best shrimp recipe! Flavorful shrimp are coated in a perfectly crispy coconut breading and then fried. You've got to try this one.

Vegetable oil, for frying

2 cups all-purpose flour

2¼ teaspoons RTB Cajun Seasoning, divided

1 teaspoon kosher salt

1 teaspoon ground black pepper

3 large eggs

1 (14-ounce) bag sweetened flaked coconut

2 cups panko (Japanese bread crumbs)

2 pounds peeled and deveined (tails left on) fresh jumbo shrimp

½ stick (¼ cup) unsalted butter, melted

1 teaspoon bottled minced garlic

½ teaspoon dried parsley

¼ teaspoon paprika

Lemon wedges, to serve

1 In a large deep skillet, pour oil to fill halfway, and heat over medium-high heat until a deep-fry thermometer registers 350°.

2 Line a baking sheet with wax paper. Line another baking sheet with several paper towels, and place a wire rack on top.

3 In a medium bowl, whisk together flour, 1 teaspoon RTB Cajun Seasoning, salt, and pepper. In another medium bowl, whisk together eggs and 1 teaspoon RTB Cajun Seasoning until lightly beaten. In a third medium bowl, stir together coconut and bread crumbs. Working in batches, dredge shrimp in flour mixture. Dip in egg mixture, letting excess drip off. Dredge shrimp in coconut mixture, pressing to adhere. Place on wax paper-lined baking sheet.

4 Fry shrimp in batches until golden brown, about 2 minutes per side. Remove from oil, and let drain on prepared wire rack.

5 In a small bowl, whisk together melted butter, garlic, parsley, paprika, and remaining ¼ teaspoon RTB Cajun Seasoning. Serve shrimp hot with butter mixture and lemon wedges.

PORK TACOS

MAKES 15 TO 18 SERVINGS

I made this recipe as part of my affordable meals series on social media. Tacos are a great way to feed a crowd for cheap.

1 stick (½ cup) unsalted butter

5 pounds pork loin, cut into 1-inch cubes

3 tablespoons olive oil

3 tablespoons RTB Dubba-U Sauce

2 (1-ounce) packages taco seasoning

½ teaspoon ground black pepper

1 medium yellow onion, diced

1 (20-ounce) can pineapple tidbits

30 to 35 (6-inch) corn tortillas

Chopped fresh cilantro, lime wedges, and chopped yellow onion, to serve

1 Preheat an outdoor flattop griddle over medium heat. Add butter. When butter melts, add pork, oil, and RTB Dubba-U Sauce. Season with taco seasoning and pepper. Cook until lightly browned, about 15 minutes, stirring frequently. Push pork to one side of griddle.

2 Add diced onion to other side of griddle. Cook until lightly browned, about 10 minutes, stirring occasionally. Stir together diced onion, pork, and pineapple. Push pork mixture to one side of griddle.

3 Add tortillas to other side of griddle; cook until heated through, 1 to 2 minutes per side. Serve pork mixture on tortillas with cilantro, lime wedges, and chopped onion.

TERIYAKI STEAK STIR-FRY

MAKES 8 SERVINGS

Have some leftover rice? This recipe is a great way to reuse it with brand-new seasonings.

1 stick (½ cup) unsalted butter

2 cups fresh broccoli florets

1½ teaspoons kosher salt, divided

1½ teaspoons ground black pepper, divided

1 teaspoon RTB Cajun Seasoning, divided

¼ cup water

1 medium green bell pepper, sliced

1 medium orange bell pepper, sliced

3 tablespoons soy sauce, divided

1 pound rib eye steak, cut into ¼-inch strips

3 teaspoons teriyaki sauce, divided

1 teaspoon garlic powder

1 teaspoon onion powder

¼ teaspoon crushed red pepper

2 cups cooked white rice, cold

2 teaspoons toasted sesame seeds

1 Preheat an outdoor flattop griddle over medium heat. Add butter. When butter melts, add broccoli to one side of griddle. Season with ½ teaspoon salt, ½ teaspoon black pepper, and ½ teaspoon RTB Cajun Seasoning. Pour ¼ cup water over broccoli. Cover and cook until tender, about 5 minutes.

2 While broccoli cooks, add bell peppers to other side of griddle. Season with 1 tablespoon soy sauce, ½ teaspoon salt, ½ teaspoon black pepper, and remaining ½ teaspoon RTB Cajun Seasoning. Push bell peppers to the side. Add steak. Season with 1 tablespoon soy sauce, 1½ teaspoons teriyaki sauce, garlic powder, onion powder, crushed red pepper, remaining ½ teaspoon salt, and remaining ½ teaspoon black pepper. Cook until browned, 4 to 5 minutes, stirring frequently. Push to back of griddle.

3 Add rice, remaining 1 tablespoon soy sauce, and remaining 1½ teaspoons teriyaki sauce to griddle. Stir together rice, broccoli, bell peppers, and steak. Sprinkle with toasted sesame seeds.

RALPH'S TIP

When I'm cooking on my griddle, I like to prep all my ingredients, especially the vegetables, ahead of time to make things go faster.

HONEY-GARLIC PORK CHOPS

MAKES 4 TO 6 SERVINGS

Thinly sliced, well-seasoned pork chops are lightly fried until crispy and then topped with parsley, salt, and lemon juice for even more flavor.

8 boneless pork chops (½ inch thick)

2 teaspoons honey garlic seasoning

2 teaspoons RTB Cajun Seasoning

¾ cup all-purpose flour

1 stick (½ cup) unsalted butter

¼ cup vegetable oil

2 tablespoons chopped fresh parsley

½ teaspoon kosher salt

Lemon wedges, to serve

1 Preheat an outdoor flattop griddle over high heat.

2 Season pork chops with honey garlic seasoning and RTB Cajun Seasoning.

3 On a plate, place flour. Dredge seasoned pork chops in flour until well coated.

4 Add butter and oil to griddle. When butter melts, add coated pork chops, and cook until a meat thermometer registers an internal temperature of 145°, 4 to 5 minutes per side. Sprinkle with parsley and salt. Serve hot with lemon wedges.

GRIDDLE BOAT TACOS

MAKES 8 SERVINGS

Griddle boats are an easy way to cook dinner. Serve with some tortillas for the perfect taco.

1½ pounds smoked sausage, sliced

1½ pounds sirloin steak, cubed

1½ pounds peeled and deveined medium fresh shrimp

1 (20-ounce) can pineapple chunks, drained

3 cups grape tomatoes

3 cups red bell pepper strips

3 cups sliced yellow onion

1 cup RTB Dubba-U Sauce

2 tablespoons RTB Cajun Seasoning

2 teaspoons kosher salt

2 teaspoons onion powder

2 teaspoons garlic powder

2 teaspoons ground black pepper

1 stick (½ cup) unsalted butter

8 (8-inch) flour tortillas

1 Preheat an outdoor flattop griddle over medium heat. Cut 8 sheets of heavy-duty foil about 12 inches long.

2 To make a foil packets, fold long edges of foil in half. Fold short edges twice to seal ends. Repeat until 8 packets are formed. Divide sausage, steak, shrimp, pineapple, tomatoes, bell pepper, and onion among foil packets. Add 2 tablespoons RTB Dubba-U Sauce to each packet, and season with RTB Cajun Seasoning, salt, onion powder, garlic powder, and pepper. Add 1 tablespoon butter to each packet; seal packets.

3 Place packets on griddle. Cook until bubbly, 15 to 18 minutes.

4 Warm tortillas on griddle, and serve hot with meat and vegetables.

BLACKENED CHICKEN STUFFED WITH CRAWFISH AND CRAWFISH FRIED RICE

MAKES 4 SERVINGS

This one is country star-approved! Tim McGraw stitched this recipe on TikTok and said he'd take two.

2 sticks (1 cup) unsalted butter, divided

½ cup diced celery

1 medium yellow onion, diced

1 medium red bell pepper, diced

1 pound crawfish tails

2 tablespoons RTB Dubba-U Sauce, divided

½ cup shredded Colby-Jack cheese blend

½ cup shredded mozzarella cheese

4 large boneless skinless chicken breasts

1 tablespoon RTB Blackened Seasoning

4 cups cooked yellow rice

1 tablespoon RTB Cajun Seasoning

1 Preheat an outdoor flattop griddle over medium heat. Add 1 stick (½ cup) butter. When butter melts, add celery, onion, and bell pepper, and cook until softened, 5 to 7 minutes, stirring occasionally. Add crawfish and 1 tablespoon RTB Dubba-U Sauce, stirring to combine. Place half of crawfish mixture in a bowl, and set aside.

2 To remaining crawfish on griddle, add cheeses, stirring to combine.

3 Slice each chicken breast lengthwise in its side but not completely through, making a pocket for the stuffing. Stuff cheesy crawfish mixture into pockets. Season both sides of chicken with RTB Blackened Seasoning.

4 Add remaining 1 stick (½ cup) butter to griddle. When butter melts, add chicken to one side of griddle. Cover and cook until a meat thermometer registers an internal temperature of 165°, 10 to 15 minutes, turning once halfway through cooking.

5 While chicken cooks, add yellow rice to other side of griddle. Stir in reserved crawfish mixture, RTB Cajun Seasoning, and remaining 1 tablespoon RTB Dubba-U Sauce. Serve rice alongside chicken.

SMOTHERED PORK CHOPS

MAKES 8 SERVINGS

Delicious pork chops are seasoned to perfection, smothered in a rich onion gravy, and served over rice.

⅓ cup peanut butter-colored Roux (recipe on page 60)

1½ cups chopped yellow onion

1½ cups chopped celery

1½ cups chopped green bell pepper

1 stick (½ cup) unsalted butter

8 bone-in pork chops (about ¾ inch thick)

1 tablespoon RTB Cajun Seasoning

2 teaspoons onion powder

2 teaspoons garlic powder

Kosher salt and ground black pepper, to taste

2 tablespoons RTB Dubba-U Sauce

8 cups chicken broth

1 large white onion, thinly sliced

2 tablespoons minced garlic

2 dried bay leaves

2 teaspoons dried parsley

Hot cooked rice, to serve

1 In a large heavy-duty skillet, cook Roux, yellow onion, celery, and bell pepper over medium heat until softened, 3 to 4 minutes, stirring frequently. Remove from heat.

2 In a cast-iron Dutch oven, melt butter over medium-high heat.

3 Season both sides of pork chops with RTB Cajun Seasoning, onion powder, garlic powder, and salt and pepper to taste. Add seasoned pork chops to pot, and cook until lightly browned, 4 to 5 minutes per side. Pour RTB Dubba-U Sauce over pork chops, and remove from Dutch oven. Set aside.

4 Add roux mixture to Dutch oven; stir in chicken broth. Add white onion and garlic. Taste and adjust seasonings if needed. Add reserved pork chops, bay leaves, and parsley. Bring to a gentle boil over medium-high heat. Cover; reduce heat to medium-low, and simmer until pork is tender and gravy is thickened, about 1½ hours. Serve hot over rice.

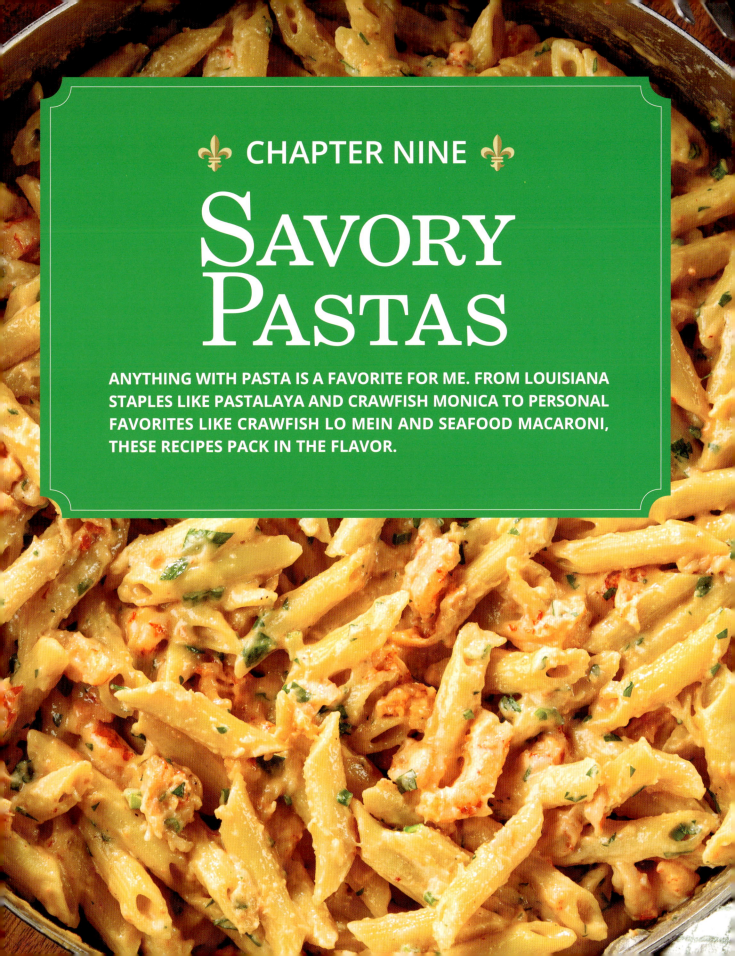

CHAPTER NINE

SAVORY PASTAS

ANYTHING WITH PASTA IS A FAVORITE FOR ME. FROM LOUISIANA STAPLES LIKE PASTALAYA AND CRAWFISH MONICA TO PERSONAL FAVORITES LIKE CRAWFISH LO MEIN AND SEAFOOD MACARONI, THESE RECIPES PACK IN THE FLAVOR.

BLACKENED ALLIGATOR AND CHEESY PASTA

MAKES 12 SERVINGS

I love alligator any way you cook it, but there is something about alligator tossed in a cheesy sauce that keeps me coming back for more.

2 sticks (1 cup) garlic and herb butter, divided

4 pounds boneless alligator meat, cut into 1-inch cubes

2 tablespoons RTB Blackened Seasoning

½ teaspoon kosher salt

½ teaspoon ground black pepper

2 pounds rotini, cooked according to package directions

3 cups heavy whipping cream, divided

1 cup shredded mild Cheddar cheese

1 cup shredded smoked Gouda cheese with bacon

1 cup chopped fresh parsley

5 cloves garlic, minced

1 lemon, zested

1 cup freshly grated Parmesan cheese

3 tablespoons RTB Dubba-U Sauce

1 Preheat an outdoor flattop griddle over medium heat. Add ½ stick (¼ cup) butter. When butter melts, add alligator, RTB Blackened Seasoning, salt, and pepper. Cook until a meat thermometer registers an internal temperature of 165°, stirring frequently. Push alligator to one side of griddle.

2 Add 1 stick (½ cup) butter to other side of griddle. When butter melts, add rotini. Stir in 2 cups cream, Cheddar, Gouda, and remaining ½ stick (¼ cup) butter. Add parsley, garlic, lemon zest, and remaining 1 cup cream, stirring to combine. Form a hole in center of rotini mixture. Top with alligator, Parmesan, and RTB Dubba-U Sauce, stirring to combine. Serve hot.

LOBSTER AND SAUSAGE PASTA

MAKES 6 SERVINGS

**This recipe adds some flair to your usual pasta dinner. Buttery lobster is
paired with savory sausage for a creamy, spicy dish.**

9 lobster tails

2 sticks (1 cup) garlic and herb butter, divided

2 teaspoons RTB Cajun Seasoning, divided

1 teaspoon kosher salt, divided

¾ teaspoon ground black pepper, divided

3 cups grape tomatoes, halved

2 pounds smoked sausage, sliced

2 teaspoons garlic powder

1 pound spaghetti, cooked according to package directions

1 cup whole milk

1 bunch fresh parsley, chopped

1 cup sliced green onion

½ cup minced garlic

2 tablespoons fresh lemon juice

Lemon wedges, to serve

1 Preheat an outdoor flattop griddle over medium heat.

2 Starting at tail fin, cut each lobster tail down center of top shell. Place palm of hand on top of lobster tail; gently press. Pull lobster meat partially through top of shell, stopping at tail fin. Do not remove meat from shell.

3 Add 1 stick (½ cup) butter to one side of griddle. When butter melts, add lobster tails. Season with 1 teaspoon RTB Cajun Seasoning, ½ teaspoon salt, and ½ teaspoon pepper. Cover and cook just until shells are bright red and meat is cooked through, about 4 minutes. Remove meat from 3 shells, and coarsely chop meat.

4 While lobster cooks, add ½ stick (¼ cup) butter to other side of griddle. Add tomatoes. Season with remaining ½ teaspoon salt and remaining ¼ teaspoon pepper. Cook until softened, stirring frequently.

5 Add sausage to griddle. Cook until lightly browned, stirring occasionally.

6 Add remaining ½ stick (¼ cup) butter to griddle. Add chopped lobster. Season with garlic powder and remaining 1 teaspoon RTB Cajun Seasoning.

7 Add spaghetti to griddle. Pour milk over spaghetti. Top with parsley, green onion, minced garlic, and lemon juice. Stir together chopped lobster, tomatoes, sausage, and spaghetti. Serve hot with lemon wedges and remaining 6 lobster tails.

SEAFOOD MACARONI

MAKES 8 TO 10 SERVINGS

If you've been looking for a good seafood macaroni and cheese recipe, I got you. This can't be beat! Not only is it cheesy but it's also full of delicious seafood and topped with crispy pork rinds for the perfect bite.

¼ stick plus 2 tablespoons unsalted butter, divided

3 cups shredded Colby-Jack cheese blend, divided

2 cups shredded part-skim mozzarella

1 cup shredded Pepper Jack cheese

1 cup heavy whipping cream

¼ cup sour cream

2 teaspoons RTB Cajun Seasoning, divided

1½ teaspoons kosher salt, divided

1½ teaspoons garlic powder, divided

1½ teaspoons onion powder, divided

1½ teaspoons paprika, divided

1 teaspoon ground black pepper, divided

1 pound peeled and deveined medium fresh shrimp

1 pound cooked crawfish tail meat

½ cup chopped yellow onion

½ cup chopped celery

½ cup chopped green bell pepper

¼ cup evaporated milk

1 pound elbow macaroni, cooked according to package directions

1 cup crushed fried pork rinds

1 Preheat an outdoor flattop griddle over medium heat. Place a 12-inch cast-iron skillet on one side of griddle. Add ¼ stick (2 tablespoons) butter to skillet. When butter melts, add 2 cups Colby-Jack, mozzarella, Pepper Jack, cream, sour cream, 1 teaspoon RTB Cajun Seasoning, 1 teaspoon salt, 1 teaspoon garlic powder, 1 teaspoon onion powder, 1 teaspoon paprika, and ½ teaspoon pepper. Cook until blended and cheese melts, about 7 minutes, stirring occasionally.

2 While cheese sauce cooks, add remaining ½ stick (¼ cup) butter to other side of griddle. When butter melts, add shrimp, crawfish, onion, celery, bell pepper, evaporated milk, remaining 1 teaspoon RTB Cajun Seasoning, remaining ½ teaspoon salt, remaining ½ teaspoon garlic powder, remaining ½ teaspoon onion powder, remaining ½ teaspoon paprika, and remaining ½ teaspoon pepper. Cook until shrimp are pink and firm, about 5 minutes, stirring frequently. Stir shrimp mixture and macaroni into cheese sauce. Top with remaining 1 cup Colby-Jack and pork rinds. Cover and cook until bubbly, 12 to 14 minutes. Serve hot.

CHEESY CRAWFISH PASTA

MAKES 12 SERVINGS

I love to make this in February and March during crawfish season, but if you're craving it later in the year, you can always use frozen crawfish tails! It works just as well.

2 sticks (1 cup) unsalted butter, divided

2 pounds cooked crawfish tail meat

1 tablespoon RTB Cajun Seasoning

2 teaspoons garlic powder

2 teaspoons dried parsley

½ teaspoon ground black pepper

2 pounds bowtie pasta, cooked according to package directions

2 cups heavy whipping cream

2 (5-ounce) packages shaved Parmesan cheese

1 Preheat an outdoor flattop griddle over medium heat. Add 1 stick (½ cup) butter. When butter melts, add crawfish, RTB Cajun Seasoning, garlic powder, parsley, and pepper, stirring to combine. Push crawfish to one side of griddle.

2 Add remaining 1 stick (½ cup) butter to other side of griddle. When butter melts, add pasta and cream, stirring to combine. Sprinkle cheese over pasta. Taste and adjust seasonings if needed. Stir pasta and crawfish together until combined. Serve hot.

PASTALAYA

MAKES ABOUT 12 SERVINGS

*Jambalaya's pasta cousin, this dish is full of all the Cajun flavor
that people love, now in a creamy pasta dish.*

½ stick (¼ cup) unsalted butter

3 stalks celery, diced

1 medium yellow onion, diced

1 medium red bell pepper, diced

1 medium green bell pepper, diced

1 bunch green onion, diced

2 pounds boneless skinless
   chicken breasts, cubed

1 pound smoked sausage, sliced

3 tablespoons minced garlic

1 tablespoon RTB Cajun Seasoning

1 teaspoon onion powder

1 teaspoon garlic powder

½ teaspoon ground black pepper

2 (32-ounce) containers chicken broth

1 (14.5-ounce) can diced tomatoes

Kosher salt, to taste

1 pound rotini pasta

1 In a large cast-iron Dutch oven, melt butter over medium heat. Add celery, yellow onion, bell peppers, and green onion. Cook until vegetables are softened, about 10 minutes, stirring occasionally. Add chicken, sausage, minced garlic, RTB Cajun Seasoning, onion powder, garlic powder, and pepper. Cook until chicken and sausage are lightly browned, 10 to 15 minutes, stirring occasionally.

2 Add chicken broth and tomatoes to chicken mixture, stirring well. Season with salt to taste. Add pasta, stirring well. Bring to a boil. Cover, reduce heat, and simmer until pasta is tender and sauce is creamy, 35 to 40 minutes, stirring frequently. Serve hot.

CHICKEN MARGHERITA PASTA

MAKES 6 SERVINGS

**I don't always love a margherita pizza, but I love those flavors in a pasta dish.
The tomatoes and pesto blend well with the spicy chicken and creamy pasta.**

2 sticks (1 cup) unsalted butter, divided

6 boneless skinless chicken breast halves

2 tablespoons dried parsley, divided

1 tablespoon plus ½ teaspoon salt, divided

1 tablespoon garlic powder

1 tablespoon RTB Cajun Seasoning

1 tablespoon ground black pepper

1 pound fettuccine, cooked according to package directions

2 cups heavy whipping cream

1 pound shredded Parmesan cheese

2 cups grape tomatoes, halved

12 slices part-skim mozzarella

1½ cups prepared basil pesto

1 Preheat an outdoor flattop griddle over medium heat. Add 1 stick (½ cup) butter to one side of griddle. When butter melts, add chicken. Season with 1 tablespoon parsley, 1 tablespoon salt, garlic powder, RTB Cajun Seasoning, and pepper. Cook until lightly browned and a meat thermometer registers an internal temperature of 165°, 5 to 10 minutes per side.

2 When chicken is almost done, add remaining 1 stick (½ cup) butter to other side of griddle. When butter melts, add fettuccine, cream, Parmesan, and remaining 1 tablespoon parsley, turning with a large metal spatula until combined and cheese melts. Remove fettuccine mixture from griddle.

3 Add tomatoes to griddle, and season with remaining ½ teaspoon salt. Cook until heated through, stirring occasionally.

4 Top chicken with mozzarella. When cheese melts, top with pesto. Serve chicken over fettuccine mixture; top with tomatoes.

RALPH'S TIP

It might not be how you're used to making pasta, but griddle pasta is an easy way to make a delicious dinner for your whole family. If you don't have a griddle, you can always make it in a cast-iron skillet! I love using both.

CRAWFISH LO MEIN

MAKES 8 SERVINGS

Everyone grab their chopsticks for my Cajun twist on a takeout classic.

1 stick (½ cup) unsalted butter

2 pounds cooked crawfish tail meat

1 large yellow onion, sliced

4 cups thinly sliced green cabbage

2 cups bean sprouts

1 cup shredded carrot

4 tablespoons soy sauce, divided

2 tablespoons minced garlic

2 tablespoons rice wine*, divided

½ teaspoon kosher salt

½ teaspoon ground black pepper

2 pounds lo mein noodles, cooked according to package directions

2 tablespoons oyster sauce

⅓ cup chopped green onion

1 Preheat an outdoor flattop griddle over medium heat. Add butter. When butter melts, add crawfish, yellow onion, cabbage, bean sprouts, carrot, 2 tablespoons soy sauce, garlic, 1 tablespoon rice wine, salt, and pepper. Cook until vegetables are almost tender (there should still be some crunch), 4 to 5 minutes, stirring frequently. Push vegetable mixture to one side of griddle.

2 Add noodles, oyster sauce, green onion, remaining 2 tablespoons soy sauce, and remaining 1 tablespoon rice wine to other side of griddle. Stir noodle and vegetable mixtures together until well combined. Serve hot.

*I use Shaoxing.

CHICKEN TORTELLINI

MAKES 6 SERVINGS

Cajun-style chicken adds heat to this bright pasta dish. Make sure you season the chicken all over and brown it well for the best flavor.

2 pounds boneless skinless chicken thighs, cut into 1-inch cubes

¾ cup Italian dressing, divided

1 stick (½ cup) unsalted butter

1 medium yellow onion, diced

5 cloves garlic, diced

2 cups cherry tomatoes

2 teaspoons kosher salt, divided

1 teaspoon ground black pepper, divided

2 teaspoons RTB Cajun Seasoning

6 cups refrigerated tortellini, cooked according to package directions

1 (8-ounce) jar roasted red peppers, drained and chopped

2 cups fresh spinach

½ cup freshly grated Parmesan cheese

1 In a large bowl, combine chicken and ½ cup Italian dressing, tossing to coat. Cover and refrigerate for 2 hours.

2 Preheat an outdoor flattop griddle over medium heat. Add butter. When butter melts, add onion and garlic. Cook until tender, about 5 minutes, stirring occasionally. Add tomatoes, and season with 1 teaspoon salt and ½ teaspoon pepper. Cook until heated through, about 2 minutes, stirring occasionally. Push to one side of griddle.

3 While vegetables cook, remove chicken from marinade, and add to other side of griddle. Discard marinade. Season with RTB Cajun Seasoning, and cook until a meat thermometer registers an internal temperature of 165°, 10 to 12 minutes, stirring occasionally. Stir together chicken, onion mixture, tortellini, red peppers, spinach, cheese, remaining ¼ cup Italian dressing, remaining 1 teaspoon salt, and remaining ½ teaspoon pepper. Serve hot.

CHICKEN ALFREDO

MAKES 6 SERVINGS

Sometimes my kids love a classic pasta dish. I usually double this recipe when I want to feed a crowd.

2 sticks (1 cup) unsalted butter, divided

3 boneless skinless chicken breasts, halved

2 tablespoons onion powder

1 tablespoon plus 1½ teaspoons RTB Cajun Seasoning, divided

1 tablespoon garlic powder

4 cups heavy whipping cream

½ cup chopped fresh parsley, divided

1 tablespoon minced garlic

12 ounces shredded Parmesan cheese

1 pound fettuccine, cooked according to package directions

1 Preheat an outdoor flattop griddle over medium heat. Add 1 stick (½ cup) butter to one side of griddle. When butter melts, add chicken. Season with onion powder, 1 tablespoon RTB Cajun Seasoning, and garlic powder. Cook until lightly browned and a meat thermometer registers an internal temperature of 165°, about 5 minutes per side.

2 While chicken cooks, place a 12-inch cast-iron skillet on other side of griddle. Add remaining 1 stick (½ cup) butter to skillet. When butter melts, add cream, ¼ cup parsley, garlic, and remaining 1½ teaspoons RTB Cajun Seasoning. Stir in cheese. Cook until thickened and cheese melts, 4 to 5 minutes, stirring constantly. Serve chicken over fettuccine; top with cheese sauce and remaining ¼ cup parsley.

In 2020, I was gaining popularity on TikTok, but I was frustrated with the platform. At the time, it was hard to respond to comments, and the videos were too short. I started a YouTube channel for more freedom. Within a few months, I received my Silver Play Button for hitting 100K subscribers. Not too long after, I received a Gold Play Button for hitting 1 million. I keep it hanging on a wall in my house, and I'm proud of the community that grew from my YouTube channel—lots of great people who've been supporting me for a long time now.

CRAWFISH MONICA

MAKES 6 TO 8 SERVINGS

This spicy crawfish dish is a staple at New Orleans Jazz Fest. Everyone always eats at least one bowl!

½ cup Blond Roux (recipe on page 60)

2 cloves garlic, minced

1 cup heavy whipping cream

1 cup whole milk

½ cup freshly grated Parmesan cheese

1 teaspoon RTB Cajun Seasoning, or to taste

1 pound crawfish tail meat

Kosher salt and ground black pepper, to taste

¼ cup chopped green onion

¼ cup chopped fresh parsley

1 pound pasta (penne or fettuccine works well), cooked according to package directions

Lemon wedges, to serve

1 In a large skillet or saucepan, add Blond Roux and garlic. Cook over medium heat until garlic is fragrant and roux is golden brown, 2 to 3 minutes, stirring constantly. Slowly pour in cream and milk, whisking constantly to avoid lumps. Bring to a simmer, stirring constantly; cook until it thickens, stirring constantly. Add cheese and RTB Cajun Seasoning, stirring until cheese melts and sauce is smooth. Stir in crawfish, and cook until heated through, 5 to 7 minutes. Season to taste with salt and pepper. Stir in green onion and parsley. Add cooked pasta, tossing to coat evenly in sauce. Squeeze lemon wedges over servings.

CRAB PASTA

MAKES 6 SERVINGS

A lot of people pair seafood with a cream-based sauce. It's delicious, but don't be afraid of tomato sauces. Red sauce is a delicious way to enjoy crab!

1 stick (½ cup) unsalted butter

2 small yellow onions

1 teaspoon crushed red pepper

12 gumbo crabs

1 cup dry white wine

½ cup bottled minced garlic

1 teaspoon kosher salt

1 teaspoon ground black pepper

1 teaspoon RTB Cajun Seasoning

3 (28-ounce) cans tomato purée

¼ cup chopped fresh parsley, plus more to serve

1 pound spaghetti, cooked according to package directions

1 In a large Magnalite pot, melt butter over medium-high heat. Add onion and crushed red pepper, and cook until tender, 5 to 6 minutes, stirring occasionally. Stir in crabs, and cook for 5 minutes. Add wine, garlic, salt, black pepper, and RTB Cajun Seasoning. Cook for 5 minutes, stirring occasionally. Add tomato purée. Fill each empty tomato can halfway with water and pour into crab mixture. Add parsley, gently stirring to combine. Cover and cook for 1 hour. Serve hot over pasta with parsley.

RALPH'S TIP

If your tomato sauce gets too thick, add a spoonful of pasta water. Not only will the pasta water help get the sauce to the texture you like but it'll also help it cling to the pasta better.

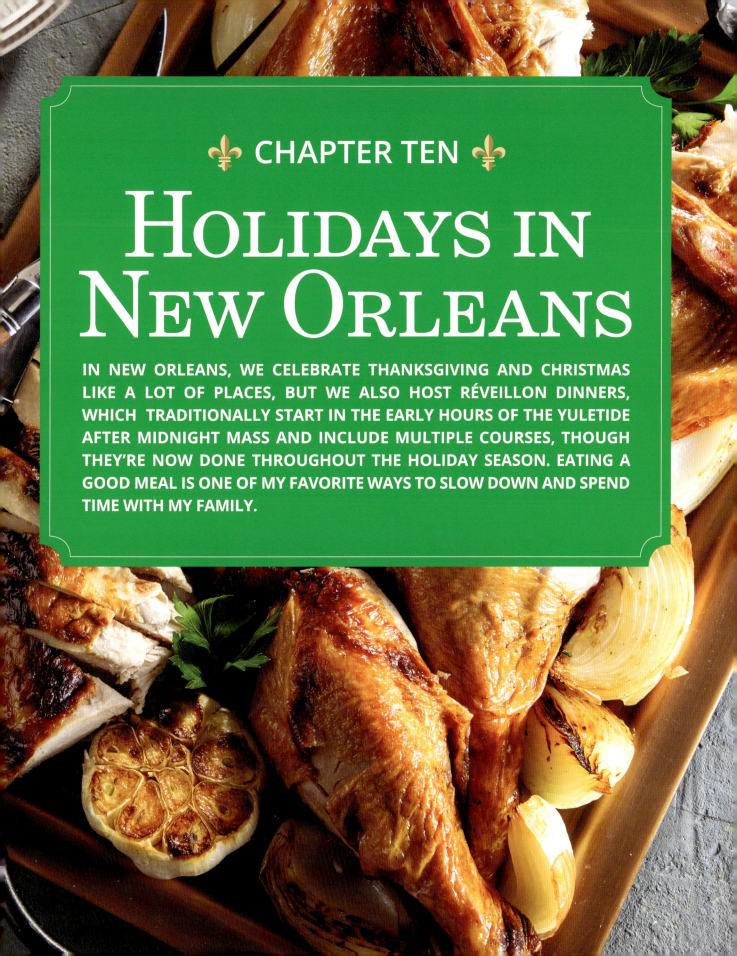

CHAPTER TEN

HOLIDAYS IN NEW ORLEANS

IN NEW ORLEANS, WE CELEBRATE THANKSGIVING AND CHRISTMAS LIKE A LOT OF PLACES, BUT WE ALSO HOST RÉVEILLON DINNERS, WHICH TRADITIONALLY START IN THE EARLY HOURS OF THE YULETIDE AFTER MIDNIGHT MASS AND INCLUDE MULTIPLE COURSES, THOUGH THEY'RE NOW DONE THROUGHOUT THE HOLIDAY SEASON. EATING A GOOD MEAL IS ONE OF MY FAVORITE WAYS TO SLOW DOWN AND SPEND TIME WITH MY FAMILY.

OYSTER DRESSING

MAKES 8 TO 10 SERVINGS

A Thanksgiving in New Orleans wouldn't be complete without my favorite Oyster Dressing.

1 tablespoon vegetable oil

1 cup chopped yellow onion

1 cup chopped celery

8 cups cubed French bread

2 tablespoons chopped fresh
  parsley, plus more for serving

3 cups oysters (oyster liquor reserved)

3 large eggs, beaten

1½ teaspoons kosher salt

1 teaspoon poultry seasoning

½ teaspoon dried thyme

¼ teaspoon ground black pepper

½ cup Italian-seasoned bread crumbs

1 Preheat oven to 325°. Spray a 2-quart baking dish with cooking spray.

2 In a large skillet, heat oil over medium-high heat. Add onion and celery, and cook until tender, about 5 minutes, stirring frequently. Mix in bread cubes and parsley, and remove from heat. Add oysters and eggs, stirring to combine. Add salt, poultry seasoning, thyme, and pepper. Stir in enough reserved oyster liquor to moisten, and mix everything thoroughly. Transfer to prepared pan. Top with bread crumbs.

3 Bake until top is toasted and a knife inserted into center comes out clean, about 45 minutes. Serve hot with parsley, if desired.

RALPH'S TIP

Drain your oysters in a colander over a large bowl. I like to stir the oysters a few times to make sure they're nice and drained.

SOUTHERN CORNBREAD

MAKES 1 (12-INCH) LOAF

This is how we make our cornbread the Cajun way. It's the perfect side to your favorite soup or stew!

1 cup all-purpose flour

1 cup fine yellow cornmeal

1 tablespoon baking powder

1 teaspoon kosher salt

1 cup whole buttermilk, room temperature

1 stick (½ cup) unsalted butter, melted

2 large eggs, room temperature

1 Preheat oven to 425°. Grease a 12-inch cast-iron skillet.

2 In a large bowl, whisk together flour, cornmeal, baking powder, and salt.

3 In a medium bowl, whisk together buttermilk, melted butter, and eggs. Add to flour mixture, stirring until just moistened. Pour batter into prepared skillet.

4 Bake until golden brown, 20 to 25 minutes. Serve warm.

Collard Greens with Ham Hocks

MAKES 6 TO 8 SERVINGS

To make traditional Southern collard greens, you have to use smoked ham hocks to flavor them. Plus, the ham hocks are great to eat alongside the greens.

2 pounds ham hocks (about 3)

1½ cups water

1 large yellow onion, diced

3 tablespoons RTB Cajun Seasoning divided

1 tablespoon bottled minced garlic

½ teaspoon kosher salt

½ teaspoon ground black pepper

2 pounds fresh collard greens, stemmed, sliced, and cleaned

1 In a large stockpot, add ham hocks, 1½ cups water, onion, 2 tablespoons RTB Cajun Seasoning, garlic, salt, and pepper over medium heat. Cover and simmer for 1 hour. Taste and adjust seasonings if needed.

2 Add half of collard greens to ham hock stock. Cook until greens are wilted, about 1 minute. Add remaining collard greens. Season with remaining 1 tablespoon RTB Cajun Seasoning. Cover and simmer until tender, about 1 hour, stirring occasionally. Serve hot.

SWEET POTATO CASSEROLE

MAKES 6 TO 8 SERVINGS

To make a real Ralph the Baker Sweet Potato Casserole, you need to arrange your marshmallows in the letters "RTB." It makes it taste better!

6 large sweet potatoes

2 sticks (1 cup) unsalted butter, softened and divided

3 cups firmly packed light brown sugar, divided

1 cup white sugar

1 (8-ounce) can evaporated milk

2 large eggs, lightly beaten

2 teaspoons ground cinnamon

1 teaspoon ground nutmeg

1 teaspoon vanilla extract

1½ cups mini marshmallows

2 cups all-purpose flour

2 cups chopped pecans

1 Preheat oven to 375°. Grease a 13x9-inch baking dish.

2 Slice each potato in half crosswise. Using a knife, poke 2 shallow holes in the skin side of each sweet potato half. Wrap in aluminum foil, and place on a baking sheet.

3 Bake until a fork easily pierces potatoes, about 1½ hours. Let stand until potatoes are cool enough to handle. Leave oven on.

4 Scoop out potato pulp into a large bowl. Discard skin. Add 1 stick (½ cup) butter, 1 cup brown sugar, white sugar, evaporated milk, eggs, cinnamon, nutmeg, and vanilla. Using a potato masher, mash until smooth. Pour mixture into prepared baking dish. Top with marshmallows.

5 In a separate bowl, mix together flour, pecans, remaining 2 cups brown sugar, and remaining 1 stick (½ cup) butter. Spoon on top of marshmallows, gently spreading until evenly coated.

6 Bake until puffed and golden brown, 20 to 30 minutes. Serve hot.

Cajun Fried Turkey

MAKES 6 TO 8 SERVINGS

This is how I make my fried turkey down here in New Orleans. It turns out juicy every time.

4 sticks (2 cups) unsalted butter

1 (7-ounce) can beer

½ cup RTB Cajun Hot Sauce

¼ cup onion juice (see note)

¼ cup garlic juice (see note)

¼ cup RTB Dubba-U Sauce

2 tablespoons ground black pepper

1 teaspoon cayenne pepper

1 (12-pound) whole turkey (see tip), neck and giblets removed

3 gallons peanut oil (or as needed)

1 In a large saucepan, melt butter over medium heat. Add beer, RTB Cajun Hot Sauce, onion juice, garlic juice, RTB Dubba-U Sauce, black pepper, and cayenne pepper; mix until well blended.

2 Using a marinade-injecting syringe or turkey baster with an injector tip, inject marinade all over turkey, including legs, back, wings, thighs, and breasts. Place in a large resealable bag, and marinate overnight in refrigerator. (Do not use a kitchen trash bag. If your turkey is large, you can use an oven bag.)

3 In a large turkey deep fryer, heat oil to 350°. Using the hanging device that comes with turkey deep fryers, slowly lower turkey into hot oil. (The turkey should be completely submerged in the oil.) Cook until a deep-fry thermometer inserted in thickest part of thigh registers 180°, 36 minutes, or 3 minutes per pound of turkey. Turn off fryer, and slowly remove turkey from oil, making sure all the oil drains out of the cavity. Let stand on a serving platter for about 20 minutes before carving. Serve warm.

NOTE: *I can find onion and garlic juice at the stores near me during the holidays. If your stores don't carry it, you can order them online.*

RALPH'S TIP

When it's time to fry, measure the amount of oil needed by lowering the turkey into the fryer and filling with enough oil to cover it. (Make sure the fryer is off.) Remove the turkey, and set aside. Make sure your turkey is completely thawed before frying. If it's still frozen when you add it to the hot oil, you could end up with a fire. Thaw the turkey!

Baked Macaroni & Cheese

MAKES 8 TO 10 SERVINGS

A lot of people like to use elbow noodles for their macaroni, but I've always loved it with long macaroni. You'll never eat it another way.

12 cups water

4½ teaspoons kosher salt, divided

16 ounces long macaroni*

2 large eggs, room temperature

⅔ cup heavy whipping cream
  (see note), room temperature

½ cup sour cream, room temperature

6 tablespoons salted butter, melted

1 teaspoon garlic powder

1 teaspoon onion powder

1 teaspoon RTB Cajun Seasoning

¼ teaspoon ground black pepper

1 (12-ounce) package shredded
  extra-sharp Cheddar cheese,
  divided

1 (8-ounce) package shredded
  Monterey Jack cheese

1 (8-ounce) block processed cheese
  product*, cubed

1 ounce shredded Parmesan cheese,
  cold

1 In a large stockpot, bring 12 cups water and 3 teaspoons salt to a boil over medium-high heat. Add macaroni, and simmer for 10 to 12 minutes. Drain macaroni; place strainer on top of pot, and place lid on top. Let stand for 40 minutes. (This will allow the macaroni to dry.)

2 Preheat oven to 400°. Lightly grease a 13x9-inch baking dish.

3 Heat a large nonstick skillet over low heat. Add eggs, cream, sour cream, melted butter, garlic powder, onion powder, RTB Cajun Seasoning, pepper, and remaining 1½ teaspoons kosher salt; whisk until combined. Add 8 ounces Cheddar, Monterey Jack, and processed cheese product; cook, stirring constantly, until cheese melts, 10 to 15 minutes. Add cooked macaroni, stirring to combine.

4 Pour macaroni mixture into prepared pan, using an offset spatula to even out top. Sprinkle Parmesan and remaining 4 ounces Cheddar on top.

5 Bake for 15 minutes. Increase oven temperature to broil. Broil for 3 minutes, checking each minute to make sure it doesn't burn. Serve warm.

If you can't find long macaroni, you can use bucatini. I use Velveeta, which cannot be shredded.

NOTE: *You can substitute the heavy whipping cream with whole milk or evaporated milk.*

RALPH'S TIP

Whole alligators can be hard to find outside of Louisiana, but you can order them online and have them shipped to your door. They ship frozen, so make sure you give yourself a day or two for the alligator to defrost.

SMOKED ALLIGATOR

MAKES 10 SERVINGS

A brined alligator stuffed with boudin and then coated in Cajun and blackened seasoning? You'll have the whole block knocking on your door as this smokes.

6 gallons water

2 cups kosher salt

1 (4-pound) whole alligator, skinned and gutted

1 cup plus 2 tablespoons RTB Cajun Seasoning, divided

2 tablespoons garlic powder

2 pounds white boudin sausage, casings removed, crumbled

1 stick (½ cup) unsalted butter, melted

⅓ cup Creole mustard

1 tablespoon RTB Blackened Seasoning

1 In a large pot, combine 6 gallons water and salt. Cook over high heat until salt dissolves. Let cool completely. (See note.) In a large container, combine salt water, alligator, 1 cup RTB Cajun Seasoning, and garlic powder. Cover and refrigerate for 24 hours. Discard brine.

2 Preheat a smoker to 250°. Add hickory chunks.

3 Using a sharp knife, split center of alligator's tail. Stuff tail with boudin. Pour melted butter and mustard over alligator; season with RTB Blackened Seasoning and remaining 2 tablespoons RTB Cajun Seasoning. Add alligator to top rack of smoker. Cover and smoke until an instant-read thermometer registers an internal temperature of 250°, 5 to 6 hours. Serve hot.

NOTE: *If your pot isn't big enough to boil 6 gallons of water at once, work in smaller batches until all salt is dissolved.*

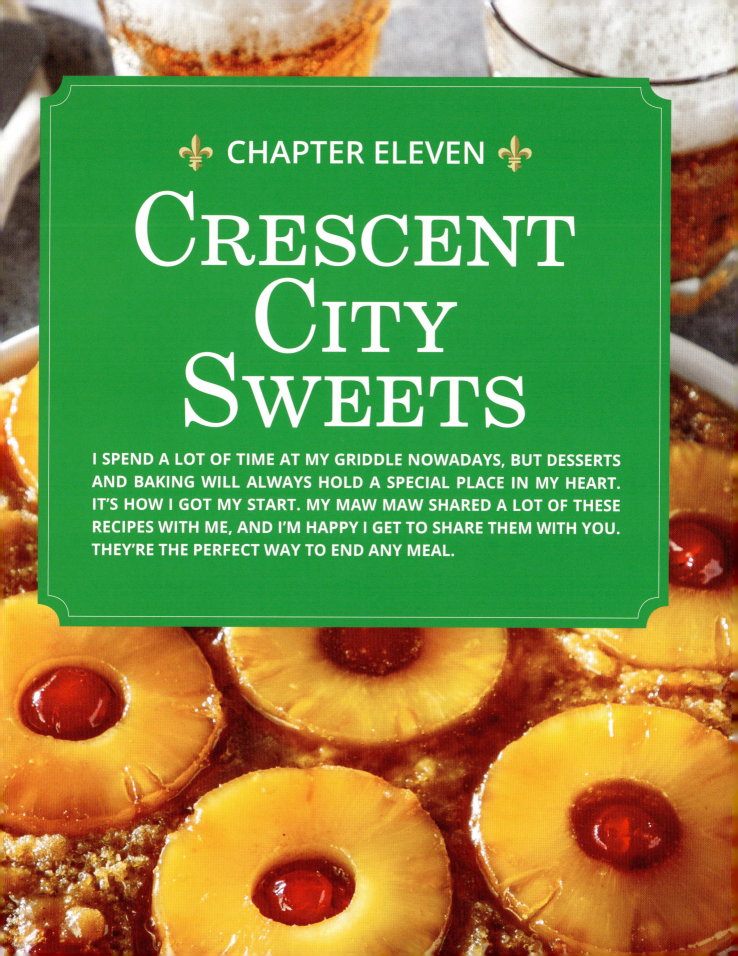

CHAPTER ELEVEN

CRESCENT CITY SWEETS

I SPEND A LOT OF TIME AT MY GRIDDLE NOWADAYS, BUT DESSERTS AND BAKING WILL ALWAYS HOLD A SPECIAL PLACE IN MY HEART. IT'S HOW I GOT MY START. MY MAW MAW SHARED A LOT OF THESE RECIPES WITH ME, AND I'M HAPPY I GET TO SHARE THEM WITH YOU. THEY'RE THE PERFECT WAY TO END ANY MEAL.

A Cooking Legacy

Growing up, I'd spend a lot of time working and fishing with my daddy, but I spent most of my time in the kitchen with Mom and Maw Maw. I loved watching them cook when I was growing up. When I was around 10, they started letting me help. They taught me all about traditional Creole and Cajun cooking and how to make something out of nothing.

As I grew up and started cooking for my own family, I took what I learned from them and applied it to new recipes. No matter what I cook, there's going to be some New Orleans flair. Cajun seasoning goes with everything!

When I started to learn to bake, I spent hours on the phone with Mom and Maw Maw. They patiently walked me through how to do so many different kinds of dishes. I think Maw Maw had to talk me through her praline recipe at least a dozen times before I finally got it right. I wouldn't trade those moments for anything. It really brought us closer together. Now, it feels like every time I cook, a part of them is with me. ⚜

Banana Pudding

MAKES 8 TO 10 SERVINGS

I like to eat my banana pudding hot, but my family likes it to be chilled. Both are delicious.

3 cups whole milk

2 (3.4-ounce) packages vanilla instant pudding mix

1 (8-ounce) package cream cheese, softened

1 (14-ounce) can sweetened condensed milk

1 (12-ounce) container frozen whipped topping, thawed

1 (11-ounce) box vanilla wafers

4 to 5 ripe bananas, sliced

1 In a large bowl, whisk together milk and pudding mix until thickened.

2 In a separate bowl, beat cream cheese with a mixer at medium speed until smooth. Add sweetened condensed milk, and beat until well combined. Add pudding mixture, and stir to combine. Fold in whipped topping.

3 In a trifle dish or serving bowl, layer vanilla wafers, bananas, and pudding mixture as desired. Cover and refrigerate for at least 4 hours before serving.

BREAD PUDDING WITH WHITE CHOCOLATE RUM SAUCE

MAKES 8 TO 10 SERVINGS

When it comes down to bread pudding, everyone likes it a little different.
I love to add raisins and cherries to mine, but my kids love it plain.

6 cups 1-inch-cubed stale bread (French bread or brioche works well)

2 cups whole milk

1½ cups heavy whipping cream, divided

4 large eggs

1¼ cups white sugar

½ stick (¼ cup) unsalted butter, melted

2 teaspoons vanilla extract

½ teaspoon ground cinnamon

¼ teaspoon ground nutmeg

½ cup raisins or chopped pecans (optional)

1 cup white chocolate chips

2 tablespoons unsalted butter

2 tablespoons rum (can substitute with ½ teaspoon rum extract)

Pinch kosher salt

Garnish: white chocolate chips, ground nutmeg

1 Preheat oven to 350°. Grease a 13x9-inch baking dish.

2 In a large bowl, combine bread cubes, milk, and 1 cup cream. Let sit for about 10 minutes, allowing bread to absorb liquid.

3 In another bowl, whisk together eggs, sugar, melted butter, vanilla, cinnamon, and nutmeg. Pour egg mixture over soaked bread cubes, and gently fold until well combined. Add raisins or pecans (if using). Transfer mixture to prepared pan, spreading evenly.

4 Bake until top is golden brown and center is set, 45 to 50 minutes.

5 In a large saucepan, cook white chocolate chips, butter, and remaining ½ cup cream until chocolate is melted and mixture is smooth, 8 to 10 minutes, stirring constantly.

6 Remove saucepan from heat, and stir in rum and salt. Serve warm bread pudding with a generous drizzle of sauce. Garnish with white chocolate chips and a sprinkle of nutmeg, if desired.

CHESS SQUARES

MAKES 15

These Southern classics are sweet and buttery. They're one of my favorite desserts to eat during the holiday season.

1 (15.25-ounce) box yellow cake mix

1 stick (½ cup) unsalted butter, melted

3 large eggs, divided

4 cups powdered sugar

1 (8-ounce) package cream cheese, softened

1 Preheat oven to 300°. Grease a 13x9-inch baking dish.

2 In a medium bowl, whisk cake mix, melted butter, and 1 egg until a soft dough forms. Press into bottom of prepared pan.

3 In another medium bowl, whisk together powdered sugar, cream cheese, and remaining 2 eggs until smooth, 1 to 2 minutes. Pour on top of crust.

4 Bake until top is golden brown, 40 to 50 minutes. Cut into squares.

RALPH'S TIP

A lot of people like to let chess squares cool completely before cutting into them. I think they taste even better when they're still warm!

PEACH COBBLER

MAKES 8 SERVINGS

This cobbler is easy to make and absolutely delicious. I love to eat it with some vanilla ice cream.

6 cups sliced fresh peaches

1 cup white sugar

2 tablespoons ground cinnamon

1 stick (½ cup) unsalted butter, melted

1 cup all-purpose flour

1 cup whole milk

2 teaspoons baking powder

1 teaspoon vanilla extract

½ teaspoon kosher salt

Vanilla ice cream, to serve

1 Preheat oven to 350°.

2 In a saucepan, combine peaches, sugar, and cinnamon. Bring to a boil over medium-high heat; reduce heat to medium-low, and simmer for 10 minutes.

3 In a 13x9-inch baking dish, pour melted butter.

4 In a bowl, stir together flour, milk, baking powder, vanilla, and salt. Pour over melted butter. Spoon peach mixture on top. Do not mix layers together.

5 Bake until top is golden brown, 40 to 45 minutes. Serve warm with ice cream.

PECAN PIE

MAKES 1 (9-INCH) PIE

A holiday classic, this pecan pie is made even better with a dash of bourbon.

1 cup light corn syrup

⅔ cup white sugar

1 stick (½ cup) unsalted butter, melted

3 large eggs

2 tablespoons bourbon

½ teaspoon kosher salt

1 cup coarsely chopped pecans

1 (9-inch) deep-dish refrigerated piecrust

1 Preheat oven to 375°.

2 In a large bowl, beat corn syrup, sugar, melted butter, eggs, bourbon, and salt with a mixer at medium speed until smooth and creamy, about 1 minute. Fold in pecans. Pour pecan mixture into piecrust. Cover edges of pie with foil to prevent excess browning, if needed.

3 Bake until center is set, about 50 minutes. Let cool slightly before serving.

RALPH'S TIP

You can enjoy this pie still warm from the oven or cooled completely. If you prefer to let it cool, let it sit at room temperature until ready to serve.

NEW ORLEANS PRALINE CANDY

MAKES 18

Whether taking them to work or putting them on your holiday table, these candies are the perfect snack for any time.

2 cups white sugar

2 cups firmly packed light brown sugar

1 cup half-and-half

½ stick (¼ cup) unsalted butter

1½ cups chopped pecans

1 In a large pot, cook sugars, half-and-half, and butter over medium heat until a candy thermometer registers 240°, stirring constantly. Remove from heat, and fold in pecans. Stir constantly until mixture thickens and loses its glossiness, 4 to 5 minutes.

2 Working quickly, spoon candy mixture by heaping tablespoonfuls onto parchment paper, and let cool completely before serving. Store in an airtight container in a cool, dry place for up to 3 weeks.

NOTE: *Humidity is pralines' worst enemy. The area that pralines are being cooked in should be pretty cool, with little to no humidity if possible. When the candy has reached 240° and you remove it from heat, the mixture can become temperamental. If humidity is too high, it can mess up the texture quickly. It is vital to begin stirring (by hand) consistently and evenly throughout the pot until the mixture loses its glossy look. It will become a peanut butter consistency when it's ready to be spooned onto parchment paper. It will give you a nice arm workout!*

LEMON BARS

MAKES 16

A buttery shortbread is topped with a tart and creamy lemon filling for the perfect zesty dessert.

2 sticks (1 cup) unsalted butter, softened

2¼ cups all-purpose flour, divided

2 cups white sugar, divided

4 large eggs, lightly beaten

2 lemons, juiced (about ½ cup)

1 Preheat oven to 350°.

2 In a medium bowl, stir together butter, 2 cups flour, and ½ cup sugar until a dough forms. Press dough evenly into the bottom of an ungreased 13x9-inch baking dish.

3 Bake until golden brown and set, 15 to 20 minutes. Let cool for at least 30 minutes. Leave oven on.

4 In another medium bowl, whisk together eggs, lemon juice, remaining 1½ cups sugar, and remaining ¼ cup flour. Pour mixture over prepared crust.

5 Bake until set, about 20 minutes. Let cool completely before cutting into squares.

PINEAPPLE UPSIDE-DOWN CAKE

MAKES 1 (12-INCH) CAKE

**For the best pineapple upside-down cake, you have to use a cast-iron skillet.
It gets the top perfectly caramelized every time.**

3 sticks (1½ cups) salted butter

1½ cups white sugar

4 large eggs

½ cup pineapple juice

½ cup cream soda*

1 teaspoon baking soda

2½ cups all-purpose flour

1 tablespoon vanilla extract

Pinch kosher salt

1 cup firmly packed light brown sugar

7 canned pineapple slices

**7 maraschino cherries,
plus more if desired**

1 Preheat oven to 350°.

2 In a 12-inch cast-iron skillet, melt butter over medium-low heat.

3 In a medium bowl, pour 1 cup melted butter. Reserve remaining butter in skillet.

4 Whisk white sugar into the 1 cup melted butter in bowl. Whisk in eggs, one at a time. Whisk in pineapple juice, cream soda, and baking soda. Add flour, vanilla, and salt, whisking to combine.

5 Add brown sugar to melted butter in skillet. Cook over medium heat until bubbly and caramelized, 4 to 5 minutes, stirring occasionally. Arrange pineapple slices in skillet, and place 1 cherry in center of each slice. Scatter any remaining cherries on top, if desired. Add batter, spreading evenly.

6 Bake until a wooden pick inserted in center comes out clean, 25 to 30 minutes. Let cool for 10 minutes. Carefully invert cake onto a plate.

*I use Big Shot Creme Soda.

Strawberry Shortcakes

MAKES 6 TO 8 SERVINGS

This is next-level strawberry shortcake! You can make it as one big dish, or you can make individual cups to serve at a party.

2 pounds fresh strawberries, sliced

½ cup white sugar

½ cup strawberry preserves

1 (14-ounce) can sweetened condensed milk

1 (8-ounce) package cream cheese, softened

1 (16-ounce) container frozen whipped topping, thawed

1 prepared angel food cake, cut into 1-inch cubes

Garnish: fresh strawberries

1 In a large bowl, stir together sliced strawberries, sugar, and preserves until combined.

2 In another large bowl, beat sweetened condensed milk and cream cheese with a mixer at medium-low speed until combined. Fold in whipped topping.

3 In small plastic cups, evenly layer half of angel food cake, half of strawberry mixture, and half of condensed milk mixture. Repeat with remaining angel food cake, remaining strawberry mixture, and remaining condensed milk mixture. Garnish with strawberries, if desired.

Sweet Potato Praline Pie

MAKES 1 (9-INCH) DEEP-DISH PIE

This pie merges two classics with the crunchy pecan layer topped with a creamy
sweet potato filling. You'll never eat sweet potato pie any other way.

1½ cups mashed cooked sweet potato

1 cup evaporated milk

½ cup white sugar

½ cup plus ⅓ cup firmly packed
   dark brown sugar, divided

3 large eggs, lightly beaten

1 teaspoon ground cinnamon

½ teaspoon kosher salt

¼ teaspoon ground nutmeg

¼ teaspoon ground cloves

All-purpose flour, for dusting

Piecrust Dough (recipe follows)

3 tablespoons unsalted butter
   or margarine, softened

⅓ cup chopped pecans

1 Preheat oven to 425°.

2 In a large bowl, add sweet potato, evaporated milk,
white sugar, ½ cup brown sugar, eggs, cinnamon, salt,
nutmeg, and cloves, whisking until smooth. Set aside.

3 Lightly dust work surface with flour, and roll Piecrust Dough
into an 11-inch circle. Fit into a 9-inch deep-dish pie plate,
and trim off excess along edges. Fold edges under, and
crimp as desired.

4 In a small bowl, stir together butter and remaining
⅓ cup brown sugar until creamy. Gently spread mixture
into crust, and sprinkle with pecans.

5 Bake on lowest oven rack for 9 minutes. Carefully open
oven, and pull out oven rack, leaving pie on rack. Pour
sweet potato filling into crust. Reduce oven temperature
to 350°, and bake until pie is set, about 40 minutes more.
Let cool completely.

Piecrust Dough

MAKES 1 (9-INCH) PIECRUST

1⅓ cups all-purpose flour

½ teaspoon kosher salt

½ cup all-vegetable shortening,
   chilled

5 to 6 tablespoons ice water

1 In a medium bowl, mix together flour and salt. Cut in
shortening with a pastry blender until mixture is crumbly.
Add 5 to 6 tablespoons ice water, 1 tablespoon at a time,
sprinkling evenly over surface, stirring with a fork until dry
ingredients are moistened. Shape into a ball.

RALPH'S TIP

To save on time, you can use a
9-inch frozen deep-dish piecrust.

BANANAS FOSTER

MAKES 4 SERVINGS

A dark rum adds to the spicy, caramel sauce coating the bananas. It's delicious with ice cream.

2 sticks (1 cup) unsalted butter

½ cup firmly packed light brown sugar

½ teaspoon ground cinnamon

1 cup banana liqueur

4 ripe but firm bananas, cut in half crosswise and lengthwise

¼ cup dark rum

Vanilla ice cream, to serve

1 In a large skillet, melt butter, brown sugar, and cinnamon over low heat until sugar dissolves, stirring constantly. Stir in liqueur. Add bananas, and cook until bananas soften and begin to brown, 1 to 2 minutes. Stir in rum, and cook until rum is hot. Tip skillet slightly to ignite rum, or ignite with a long match or stick lighter. Cook until flame dies out. Serve with ice cream.

RECIPE INDEX

BREAKFAST

Brioche French Toast with
    Praline Cream Cheese Filling **18**
Cajun Sausage Gravy **25**
Homemade Butter **29**
Louisiana Cajun Breakfast Skillet **21**
New Orleans Beignets **22**
Praline Sauce **17**
Southern Buttermilk Biscuits **26**

DESSERT

Banana Pudding **231**
Bananas Foster **251**
Bread Pudding with White Chocolate
    Rum Sauce **232**
Chess Squares **235**
Lemon Bars **243**
New Orleans Praline Candy **240**
Peach Cobbler **236**
Pecan Pie **239**
Pineapple Upside-Down Cake **244**
Strawberry Shortcakes **247**
Sweet Potato Praline Pie **248**

DIPS & SNACKS

Boudin Cheese Ball **34**
Boudin Dip **42**
Cajun Buffalo Dip **37**
Cajun Cracklings **112**
Crawfish Queso Dip **33**
Crawfish, Spinach, and Artichoke Dip **45**
Louisiana Hot Crab Dip **38**
Mexican Street Corn Nachos **135**
New Orleans Crab Cakes **85**
Pepper Jelly-Cheese Dip **99**

PORK & BEEF

Boudin King Cake **108**
Boudin King Cake Burgers **100**
Cabbage Rolls **165**
Cajun Stuffed Bell Peppers **170**
Carne Asada **131**
Fajita Bowls **120**

Griddle Boat Tacos **181**
Honey-Garlic Pork Chops **178**
New Orleans Muffuletta **90**
New Orleans Red Beans and Rice **89**
Pork Tacos **174**
Smashburgers **136**
Smothered Pork Chops **185**
Steak and Crawfish Sandwiches **119**
Steak Sliders **124**
Taco Burgers **132**
Teriyaki Steak Stir-Fry **177**
Tomahawk Steak with Shrimp **139**
Yaka Mein **93**

POULTRY

Blackened Chicken Stuffed with
    Crawfish and Crawfish Fried Rice **182**
Cajun Fried Turkey **221**
Chicken Alfredo **205**
Chicken and Shrimp Fried Rice **127**
Chicken Margherita Pasta **198**
Chicken Tortellini **202**
Fried Chicken **166**
Honey Buffalo Fried Chicken Strips **128**
Hot Wings **103**
Jambalaya **82**
Pastalaya **197**

SEAFOOD

Alligator Sauce Piquant **73**
Blackened Alligator and Cheesy Pasta **189**
Blackened Catfish **144**
Cajun Smothered Squash with Shrimp **148**
Chargrilled Oysters **104**
Cheesy Crawfish Pasta **194**
Coconut Shrimp **173**
Crab Pasta **209**
Crawfish Boil **77**
Crawfish Étouffée **74**
Crawfish Lo Mein **201**
Crawfish Monica **206**
Fried Alligator **147**
Fried Shrimp Po' Boys **115**

Frog Legs **156**
Lobster and Sausage Pasta **190**
Mini Crawfish Pies **78**
Sautéed Crab Claws **107**
Seafood Cajun Lasagna **159**
Seafood Macaroni **193**
Seafood Potatoes **155**
Shrimp and Grits **143**
Shrimp and Sausage Boats **123**
Shrimp Boil **111**
Shrimp Rémoulade **152**
Smoked Alligator **225**
Soy Sauce and Garlic Salmon and
    Vegetables **169**
Spicy Honey-Garlic Salmon **151**
Sweet and Sour Turtle **160**

SOUPS, STEWS & CHILIS

Blond Roux **60**
Cajun Chili **51**
Cajun Potato and Sausage Soup **52**
Chicken and Dumplings **59**
Corn and Crab Bisque **68**
Roux **60**
Seafood Gumbo **67**
Shrimp Stew **64**

VEGGIES, SIDES & LAGNIAPPE

Baked Macaroni & Cheese **222**
Collard Greens with Ham Hocks **217**
Creole Dirty Rice **81**
French Bread Crumbs **87**
Fried Green Tomatoes **41**
Fried Okra **55**
Garlic Bread **42**
Hush Puppies **56**
Mirliton Casserole **86**
Piecrust Dough **248**
Okra Creole **63**
Oyster Dressing **213**
Southern Cornbread **214**
Sweet Potato Casserole **218**

EDITORIAL

Founder
Phyllis Hoffman DePiano

President/Chief Creative Officer
Brian Hart Hoffman

EVP/Chief Content Officer
Brooke Michael Bell

Editorial Director
Marie Baxley

Art Director
Jodi Rankin Daniels

Senior Editor
Kristi Fleetwood

Senior Copy Editor, Food
Meg Lundberg

Test Kitchen Director
Laura Crandall

Food Stylists
Aaron Conrad, Katie Moon Dickerson, Kathleen Kanen, and Vanessa Rocchio

Senior Prop Stylist
Sidney Bragiel

Prop Stylists
Maghan Armstrong, Courtni Bodiford, Maggie Hill, and Donna Nichols

Photographers
Jim Bathie, Kyle Carpenter, and John O'Hagan

Senior Digital Imaging Specialist
Delisa McDaniel

PRODUCTION & MARKETING

President/Chief Executive Officer
Eric Hoffman

EVP/Chief Operating Officer
Greg Baugh

EVP/Chief Marketing Officer
Missy Polhemus

VP/Marketing
Kristy Harrison

Associate Marketing Manager
Morgan Barbay

ACKNOWLEDGMENTS

I extend my heartfelt gratitude to all those who have contributed to the creation of this cookbook. Your support and encouragement have been invaluable, and I'm deeply thankful for your contributions.

To my partners at 83 Press: I would like to thank your dedicated team for their unwavering support and expertise in bringing this cookbook to life. Your guidance and collaboration have been instrumental in making this project a reality.

To my children: Y'all have been an intricate part of this success. Kelly, you are always willing to help, be present, and celebrate. I'm so thankful to have you on this journey with me. Alyssa, you've played a larger role than you give yourself credit for. From helping Mom tame the chaos behind the scenes to offering a helping hand, I couldn't have done it without you. RJ, my right-hand man, my cooking partner, I'm honored to share this accomplishment with you. Preston, you encouraged me to explore different cultures in the culinary world and made me a better chef. Parker, your lightheartedness in the kitchen reminds me of the joy cooking brings to families. I'm honored to be your father. Y'all are the reason I continue to do this.

To my parents, Rose and Ralph Williams: I am eternally grateful for the love and support you've given me. Mom, you have passed down most of these recipes to me. You've answered every call and question, even retaught cooking techniques. Dad, your willingness to be a helping hand and show up for anything means the world to me. Y'all have taught me the core values of family, food, and tradition. Thank you for teaching me how our culture with food can bring families together. I wouldn't be Ralph the Baker if it weren't for y'all.

To my siblings: Y'all are my biggest cheerleaders. Melissa, you've built my confidence and never let me believe I could fail. Hope, thank you for re-creating my recipes and being astonished at how great they turned out. Also, thank you for offering your home to us for the cookbook production and the sacrifice that was. Amanda, you have been my shoulder to lean on. You'd brainstorm ideas, how to do better, and started the everlasting cooking battle with me. By the way, I'm still winning! I'm so grateful for y'all.

To my dear friends, family, and supporters: Thank you for your encouragement and enthusiasm throughout this journey. Your moral support has been essential, and I'm grateful for your presence in my life.

May this cookbook bring joy, inspiration, and delicious flavors to your tables for years to come.

With sincere appreciation,
Ralph